Domestic Smart Charging Systems

7003

National Automotive Parts Association

JONES & BARTLETT
LEARNING

World Headquarters
Jones & Bartlett Learning
5 Wall Street
Burlington, MA 01803
978-443-5000
info@jblearning.com
www.jblearning.com

National Automotive Parts Association
2999 Wildwood Parkway
Atlanta, GA 30339
800-292-6428
support@napatraining.com
https://mt.napaautotech.com
https://mt.napaautocaretraining.com

ISBN: 978-1-284-20079-9

Cover Image Credit: © Travelerpix/Shutterstock

6048

Printed in the United States of America
23 22 21 20 19   10 9 8 7 6 5 4 3 2 1

NAPA Autotech

Important Safety Precautions

Appropriate service methods and repair procedures are essential for the safe and reliable operation of all motor vehicles as well as for the personal safety of the individual doing the work. This course provides general directions for accomplishing service and repair work with tested, effective techniques. Following them will help ensure reliability.

Give special attention to the details discussed in the procedures. Observing these steps can prevent you from making a mistake that could damage a vehicle or cause personal injury.

The following general safety precautions should be followed whenever you are working on a vehicle:

- Always wear safety glasses for eye protection.
- Use safety stands whenever a procedure requires you to be under the vehicle.
- Remove keys from the ignition switch, unless otherwise required by the procedure. Always follow the manufacturer's current safety procedures. Some vehicles can autostart under certain conditions.
- Set the parking brake when working on the vehicle. If the vehicle has an automatic transmission, set it in PARK unless instructed otherwise for a specific service operation. If the vehicle has a manual transmission, it should be in REVERSE (engine OFF) or NEUTRAL (engine ON) unless instructed otherwise for a specific service operation.
- Operate the engine only in a well-ventilated area or use the ventilating system provided to avoid the danger of carbon monoxide poisoning.
- Keep yourself and your clothing away from moving parts when the engine is running, especially the fan and belts.
- To prevent serious burns, avoid contact with hot metal parts, such as the radiator, exhaust manifold, tail pipe, catalytic converter, and muffler.
- Do not smoke while working on the vehicle.
- To avoid injury, always remove rings, watches, loose-hanging jewelry, and loose clothing before beginning work on a vehicle. Tie long hair securely behind the head.
- Keep hands and other objects clear of the radiator fan blades. Electric cooling fans can start operating at any time by an increase in underhood temperatures, even if the ignition is in the OFF position. Therefore, care should be taken to ensure that the electric cooling fan is completely disconnected when working under the hood.

Disclaimer of Warranties

The information in this program is based on technical data and tests and is intended for use by persons having technical skill, at their own discretion and risk. Because the working conditions of the user are outside the control of the National Automotive Parts Association (NAPA), NAPA Autotech, NAPA Institute of Automotive Technology (NIAT), and its affiliates, NAPA, NAPA Autotech, NIAT, and its affiliates assume no liability for the use of such information or for any damages resulting from its use or application. Nothing contained in such programs and publications is to be construed as contractual or providing any form of warranty.

Public exhibition or use of this material for group training or in any training curriculum without written permission from the copyright owner is prohibited by law. This publication is a training guide and does not replace any current shop manuals. Always follow current safety and service procedures.

The NAPA 7

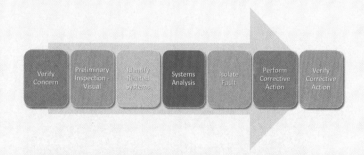

NAPA has devised a diagnostic routine to assist the technician in determining the root cause of the customer's concern. This is a systematic approach to diagnostics that can be used for any concern and represents best practices in addressing that concern. By following the NAPA 7 diagnostic approach, you can identify the problem and perform the repair without relying on trial and error. Take one step at a time and make sure of your findings before moving on.

Domestic Smart Charging Systems

Learning Objectives

Upon successful completion of this class, the attentive technician should be able to do the following:

- Identify the charging system approaches used by domestic manufacturers.
- Enhance their skill set and have a renewed approach to simplifying their diagnostic path when working on domestic charging systems.
- Demonstrate proper diagnostic approaches to isolating the root cause of charging system issues.

Introduction

Until recently the main concern when servicing the charging system was properly identifying the field type in order to polarize the regulator to match. Today's charging systems use drivers in the control module and/or bus communication networks. Gaining an understanding of how domestic manufacturers approach the charging system is key to simplifying the system. A systematic testing approach is also what doctors use to diagnose and correct the cause of a medical problem. For example, if a patient comes to a doctor with a sore throat, the first step in the diagnostic process is not likely to be exploratory surgery or a "cure it all" transplant. Instead, the doctor begins with simple tests that provide essential information. The same is true for diagnosing today's computer-controlled charging systems. As vehicle electrical systems become increasingly complex, a systematic step-by-step approach helps to ensure accurate diagnostic work and effective repairs.

Batteries

The battery is the heart of the electrical system (**FIGURE 1**). Many drivability, intermittent accessory operation, and other electrical system failures contribute to a poorly performing battery. The charging system cannot operate properly if the battery is weak or has failed.

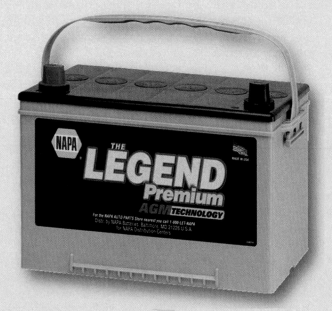

A   B

FIGURE 1 A. Flooded lead acid battery. **B.** Absorbable glass mat battery.

Battery Testing

The battery needs to be tested before performing charging system diagnostics.

State of Charge

Measuring the battery's state of charge (SOC) is a basic test for determining whether the battery is fully charged. A fully charged battery is necessary when testing the charging system. To perform the SOC test, connect a voltmeter across the battery terminals. The voltage reading is directly related to the SOC of the battery.

TABLE 1 shows the SOC based on battery voltage of a flooded lead acid (FLA) battery.

TABLE 1 FLA Battery SOC	
SOC (%)	Voltage
100	12.60+
90	12.50
80	12.42
70	12.32
60	12.20
50	12.06
40	11.90
30	11.75
20	11.58
10	11.31
0	10.50

TABLE 2 shows the SOC for an absorbable glass mat (AGM) battery. Be sure to properly identify the battery type to ensure accurate test results.

TABLE 2 AGM Battery SOC	
SOC (%)	Voltage
100	12.60+
90	12.50
80	12.42
70	12.32
60	12.20
50	12.06
40	11.90
30	11.75
20	11.58
10	11.31
0	10.50

If the SOC is low, the battery will need to be recharged before performing charging system diagnostics.

CAUTION: Do not attempt to recharge the battery if it is frozen. Let it sit until it thaws.

TECH TIP

Using a maintainer on the battery while performing diagnostics and repairs is always recommended. This will avoid straining the battery and causing diagnostic issues related to low system voltage.

Once connected, the tester can screen for battery problems as well as issues with the starting system and charging system (**FIGURE 2**).

FIGURE 2 Electronic battery testing.

With electronic testing equipment, the battery screening process should take no longer than 3 minutes to perform. This process includes visual inspection of belts, cables, and connections. Once the electronic tester is connected, the tester can screen for battery condition as well as issues with the starting and charging systems. The ability to print the test results makes the process even more effective.

A good tester should have leads that are long enough for the screening to be performed by a single technician from the vehicle's driver seat.

Conductance Testing

Many electronic battery testers measure battery conductance by sending a frequency signal through the battery while measuring frequency degradation (**FIGURE 3**). This test reveals how much plate area is available to hold and deliver power.

FIGURE 3 Midtronics CPX with conductance profiling.

Conductance declines as the battery ages. Cell defects, such as opens and shorts, also reduce conductance. This makes measuring conductance an accurate indication of battery condition.

TECH TIP

Activate the starter to load the battery during the test to get a more complete picture of overall battery health.

Most electronic battery testers analyze the cold cranking amps (CCA) capacity of the battery. This can provide an estimate of the battery's remaining service life. Some testers will also measure starter draw and analyze the charging system output.

TECH TIP

No revolutions per minute (RPM) detected by the electronic tester is a common issue in newer vehicles. Some alternators use transistors instead of diodes in the rectifier bridge. All electronic testers use the frequency of diodes to determine RPM. Because transistors do not give off the same frequency, the tester does not detect RPM. To overcome this issue, allow for 10 to 12 seconds to pass and manually push the enter button. This instructs the tester to run as a bypass and conduct the test as normal without RPM detection.

Electronic battery testers will require the inputting of battery type (**FIGURE 4**). To obtain valid test results, it is important to properly identify the battery type. Inputting the incorrect battery type into the test equipment can report a good battery as a failure.

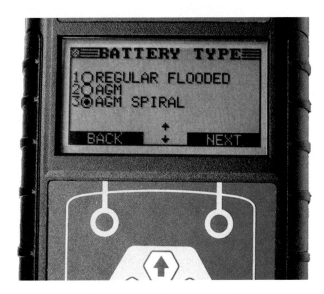

FIGURE 4 Proper battery type selection is critical.

An important aspect of obtaining proper test results is proper test lead connections. Improper test connections cause heat and skew the test results (**FIGURE 5**).

FIGURE 5 Out-of-vehicle testing adapters.

If the battery has dual post connections, use the connection that connects the battery to the vehicle.

Battery Registration

It may be necessary to perform a battery registration process (**FIGURE 6**) if the battery is replaced. This procedure stores the vehicle, resets the stored battery measurements, initializes power management functions, and allows battery capacity and type retrofit. Failure to perform the registration process may result in early battery failure.

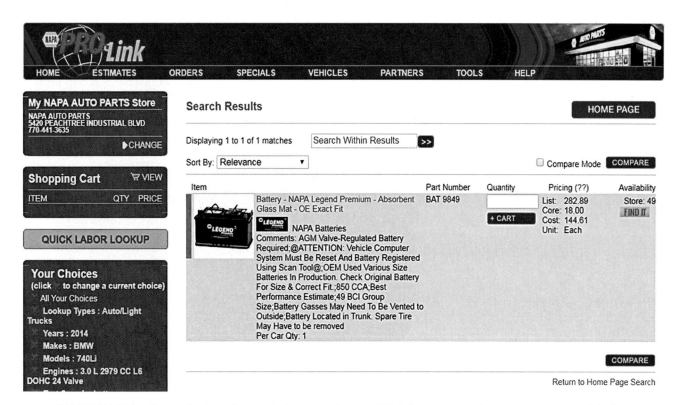

FIGURE 6 NAPA PROLink identifies applications that require battery registration. This information is in the comments section of the battery description.

Battery registration can be done using properly equipped scan tools (**FIGURE 7**). Some battery testers will also be able to register the battery.

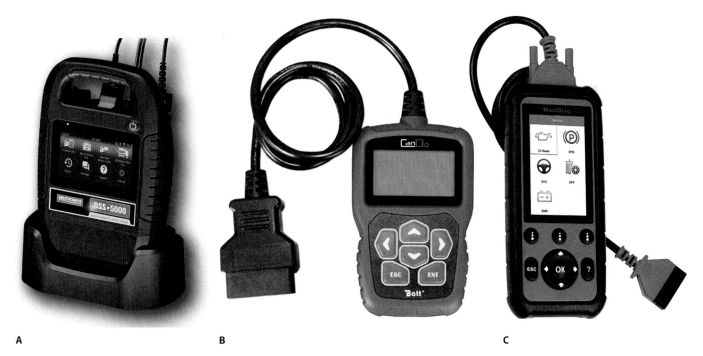

A   B   C

FIGURE 7 Three tools that have quick battery registration processes. **A.** DSS-5000. **B.** CanDo battery reset tool. **C.** Autel reset tool.

NOTES

Data Link Connector Keep-Alive Device Connections

Keep-alive memory devices prevent the loss of stored data when the battery is disconnected. Some devices plug into the data link connector (DLC). Two common styles (**FIGURE 8**) are the fully populated 16-pin connector and the 3-pin connector that provides only power and ground.

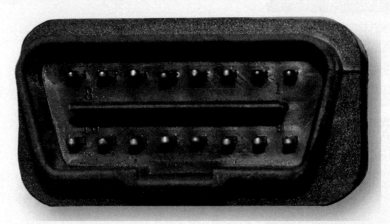

A

B

FIGURE 8 **A.** 16-pin connector. **B.** 3-pin connector.

TECH TIP

Each type of connector has some known issues. The 16-pin keep-alive cables may blow fuses on some imports, such as Honda, Acura, Mercedes-Benz, and Volvo. The 3-pin connector may not keep radio memory on mid-2000s Chrysler products, causing radio security lockout.

Charging Systems

Most alternators are belt-driven by the engine's crankshaft (**FIGURE 9**). For the alternator to produce the required current to recharge the battery and operate the accessories, the belt must be properly tensioned and in good condition.

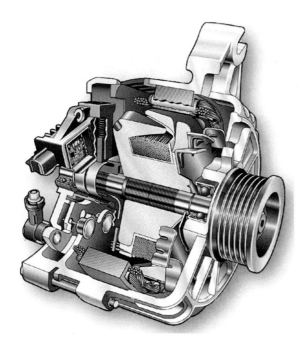

FIGURE 9 Alternator.

TECH TIP

If a vehicle has repeated alternator failures, it may be the fault of the battery. The battery may not be able to build up normal resistance as it accepts a charge. This keeps the alternator producing a higher than normal current for an extended time. The additional work causes the alternator to overheat, which eventually leads to its failure. Under proper operating conditions, charging current from the alternator should gradually decrease after the engine starts and taper off to less than 10 amps at idle with no load. If a fully charged battery requires the charging system to put out 20 or more amps after 5 minutes of idling, the battery may be defective and needs to be tested.

Belt Inspection

A simple visual inspection may not be enough to confirm if a modern drive belt is worn out to the point that a replacement is needed. Think of a serpentine belt, such as the one shown in **FIGURE 10**, as a series of "V" belts. The wear of the single V belt rib is the same as that for each rib of the serpentine belt. Like the V belt, loss of belt material increases the space between the ribs. This can cause the belt to bottom out in the pulleys, resulting in accelerated wear, belt slip, and contamination. In addition, if the belt is bottomed out and water gets onto the pulleys, it cannot channel out properly. This causes the belt to hydroplane on the water and slip.

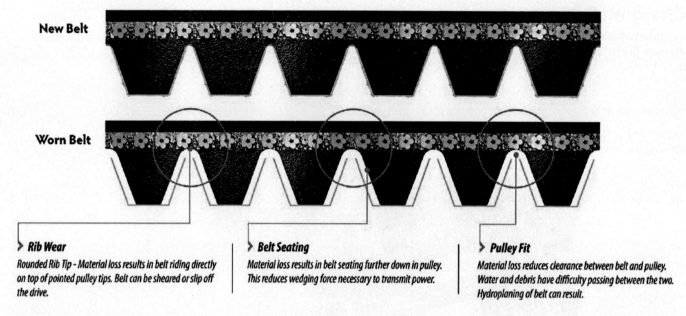

Rib Wear
Rounded Rib Tip – Material loss results in belt riding directly on top of pointed pulley tips. Belt can be sheared or slip off the drive.

Belt Seating
Material loss results in belt seating further down in pulley. This reduces wedging force necessary to transmit power.

Pulley Fit
Material loss reduces clearance between belt and pulley. Water and debris have difficulty passing between the two. Hydroplaning of belt can result.

FIGURE 10 Belt inspection.

NOTES

It doesn't take much. As little as a 5% material loss can significantly affect belt-driven component performance.

A new gauge has been developed to check for rib wear on modern belts and is much easier to use. With the engine off, press the gauge ribs into the grooves of the belt using gentle pressure to seat the ribs. Attempt to rock the gauge in a lateral motion. The belt is good if the gauge remains tightly seated and resists movement. The belt is worn out and needs to be replaced if rocking produces lateral gauge movement (**FIGURE 11**).

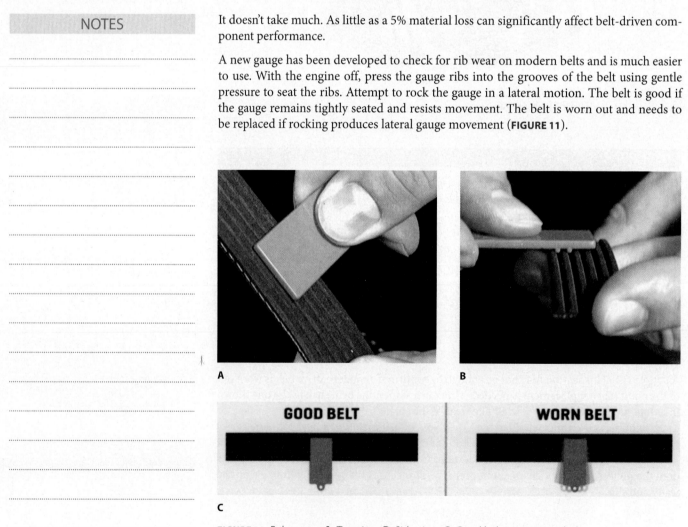

FIGURE 11 Belt gauge. **A.** Top view. **B.** Side view. **C.** Good belt versus worn belt.

Voltage Drop Testing

Voltage drop testing determines if there is excessive resistance in a charging circuit and is used to pinpoint the location of the resistance. Remember that voltage drop testing will not work unless there is current flowing in the circuit while taking the measurements. For the charging system, this means that the engine must be running at 2000 RPM and electrical loads are operating during testing. If this is not possible, use an artificial source for current flow during testing.

To determine if there is too much resistance on the positive side of the charging system circuit, start the engine and run it at 2000 RPM. Turn on as many vehicle electrical loads as possible. Set the digital volt ohm meter (DVOM) to the direct current (DC) volts scale. Place the positive meter lead on the alternator B+ terminal and the negative meter lead on the positive battery post. The reading should not be greater than 0.5 V (**FIGURE 12**).

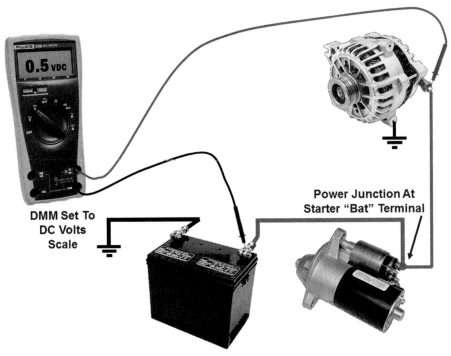

DMM Set To DC Volts Scale

Power Junction At Starter "Bat" Terminal

FIGURE 12 Voltage drop—positive cable.

This procedure tests the entire positive side of the circuit in a single step. If the reading shows excess resistance, pinpoint testing will find the actual location of the resistance.

Testing the voltage drop on the ground side of the charging system circuit is done in the same manner as the positive side. The difference is that the test leads are relocated so that the positive test lead is located at the negative battery post and the negative test lead is located on the alternator case. The reading should not exceed 0.3 V (**FIGURE 13**).

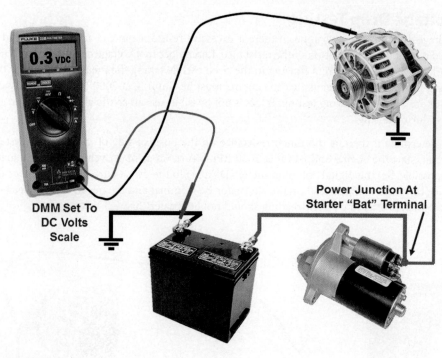

FIGURE 13 Voltage drop—ground side.

AC Ripple Voltage Test

Excessive alternating current (AC) ripple voltage not only causes poor charging system performance but also can cause drivability problems because of the effects it has on vehicle computers and computer controls. To perform the AC ripple test (**FIGURE 14**) with a DVOM, do the following:

1. Set the DVOM to the AC volts scale.
2. Start and run the engine at idle.
3. Apply a 25 amp load by turning on the headlights. Do not load more than 25 amps.
4. Place the positive meter lead on the alternator B+ terminal.
5. Place the negative meter lead on the alternator housing.
6. Observe the reading (**FIGURE 15**).

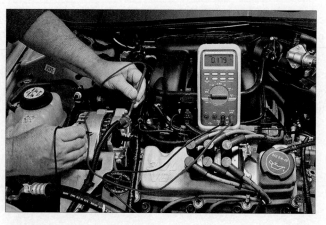

FIGURE 14 DVOM—AC ripple test.

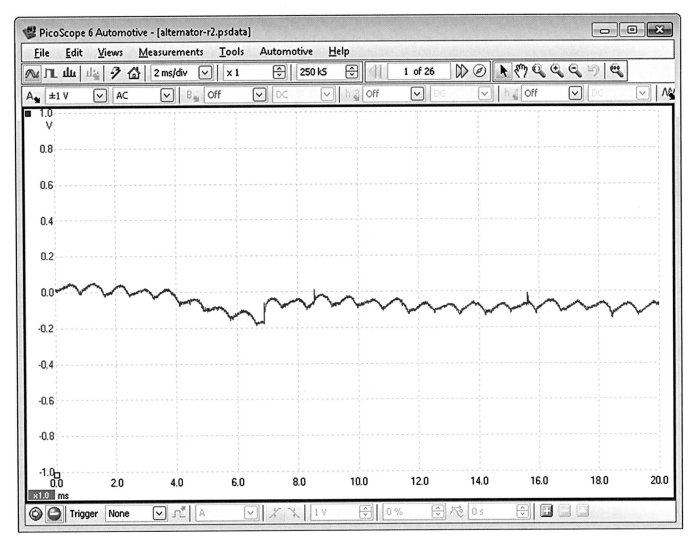

FIGURE 15 A lab scope is an excellent tool for testing AC ripple because it allows you to see every voltage change.

Take the readings at the alternator, not at the battery. The battery tends to reduce the ripple voltage, which reduces the accuracy of the test. The reading should not exceed 0.5 V AC. If it is greater than this, the alternator is defective and must be replaced.

TECH TIP

A reading between 0.2 and 0.5 V (200–500 mV) AC indicates that the alternator needs to be replaced. Newer vehicles have smaller tolerances for excessive ripple.

Parasitic Draw

There will always be some ignition-off draw (IOD) because the vehicle's computers, clocks, and radios all require some current when the vehicle is shut down. Typically, this amount of draw is between 25 and 50 milliamps. If a circuit or system fails to shut down, the IOD will become excessive and drain the battery. The customer will typically state that their battery is dead every morning.

When diagnosing for excessive IOD, look at some obvious things first, such as the glove box not closed or the underhood light staying on. If the cause is not located, then the circuits will need to be checked.

NOTES

In modern vehicle applications, pulling a fuse may cause the IOD to increase. This occurs when a computer circuit that has entered sleep mode might have been reactivated by the fuse removal. In addition, if a module is "hung up" and does not enter sleep mode, pulling the fuse removes power to the module and it may reset. Because the fuse may protect more than one module, it is more difficult to determine which one is at fault.

To isolate the circuit that has the excessive IOD, perform a voltage drop test across each of the fuses (**FIGURE 16**). Be sure to allow the control modules to power down before performing this test.

FIGURE 16 Parasitic draw test—voltage drop.

With the voltmeter on the millivolt scale, connect the test leads across the test ports of the fuse. If current is flowing through the fuse, there will be a voltage reading.

Because of the construction of each fuse rating, voltage drop readings will differ for the same amount of current. For example, a voltage drop reading of 0.8 mV across a 5 amp mini fuse means it is flowing about 50 milliamps of current. A 20 amp mini fuse will have a voltage drop reading of less than 0.2 mV for 50 milliamps of current.

If current flow through a fuse is indicated, use the wiring diagram to determine which circuits and components the fuse is protecting. Disconnect each component one at a time until the voltage drop returns to normal.

It is possible to determine the amount of current flowing in the circuit using **TABLE 3**, based on the type of fuse.

TABLE 3 Mini Fuse Voltage Drop Chart—Circuit Current across Fuse (milliamps)

Fuse Color	Gray	Violet	Pink	Tan	Brown	Red	Blue	Yellow	Clear	Green
Measurement (mV)	Mini 2 A	Mini 3 A	Mini 4 A	Mini 5 A	Mini 7.5 A	Mini 10 A	Mini 15 A	Mini 20 A	Mini 25 A	Mini 30 A
0.1	2	3	4	6	9	13	22	31	42	51
0.2	4	6	9	11	18	27	44	62	85	108
0.3	5	9	13	17	28	40	66	93	127	162
0.4	7	12	17	23	37	54	87	125	169	216
0.5	9	15	21	28	46	67	109	156	212	270
0.6	11	18	26	34	55	81	131	187	254	324
0.7	13	21	30	39	65	94	153	218	297	378
0.8	14	24	34	45	74	108	175	249	339	432
0.9	16	27	38	51	83	121	197	280	381	486
1.0	18	30	43	56	92	135	218	312	424	541
1.1	20	33	47	62	101	148	240	343	466	595
1.2	22	36	51	68	111	162	262	374	508	649
1.3	23	39	55	73	120	175	284	405	551	703
1.4	25	41	60	79	129	189	306	436	593	757

Full charts are available in the Resource section at the end of this manual.

Because current flow generates heat, a thermal imaging camera can isolate which fuse(s) has the IOD (**FIGURE 17**).

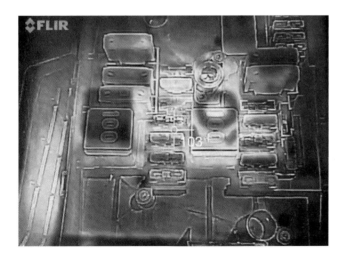

FIGURE 17 Thermal imaging.

NOTES

TECH TIP

A thermal imaging camera has several uses in automotive diagnostics and may be well worth the investment. Uses include identifying which cylinder is misfiring; heating, ventilation, and air conditioning (HVAC) diagnostics; heated seat diagnostics; and back glass defroster diagnostics.

Duty Cycle Definition

Many of today's charging systems use duty cycling of the field circuit to control alternator output. A duty cycle is defined as the proportion of time that a component, device, or system is operating. Duty cycle can be displayed as a ratio or a percentage.

Duty cycle can be measured on either the positive side of the circuit using high side drivers (HSDs) or the negative side of the circuit using low side drivers (LSDs). Be sure to set your DVOM trigger to positive or negative based on the type of control to get accurate duty cycle readings.

Scan tools usually display alternator control as a percentage. Local interconnect network (LIN) bus systems are the exception. The commanded duty cycle should increase with added loads, unless the system is in a corrective action or mode.

A lab scope allows you to see the duty cycle. **FIGURE 18** shows the duty cycle trace of a low-side controlled circuit. The field winding is activated when the voltage is low. If the scope parameters are set to 100 ms across and the low side of the pattern is only 10 ms long, the system is functioning at a 10% duty cycle. The duty cycle should increase as loads in the electrical system are applied.

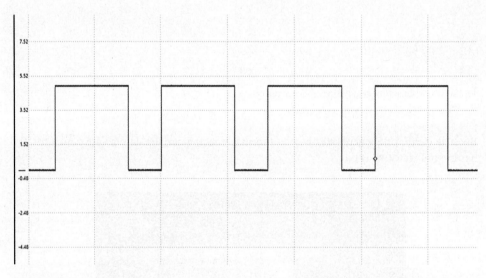

FIGURE 18 Duty cycle pattern.

When the field circuit is turned on, the voltage should go close to 0 V. However, the trace may not go completely to 0 V because there will be some voltage drop due to the transistor's turn-on voltage.

A controlled duty cycle from the positive side will activate the field when battery voltage is applied. In this case, use the high voltage readings to determine the duty cycle percentage.

GM Charging Systems

In recent years, GM has introduced regulated voltage control (RVC), which uses a different approach to charging system voltage regulation (**FIGURE 19**).

FIGURE 19 GM powertrain control module.

An alternator's field current is controlled by logic external to the alternator. Regulation is based on battery SOC and estimated battery temperature. A battery current sensor is used to monitor current flow in and out of the battery so that the system can continually respond to current demands.

The control module determines the duty cycle for the battery to maintain an SOC of 80%. Additional functions include corrective actions and load shedding.

TECH TIP

The scan tool's voltage set point and parameter ID (PID) can provide an indication of battery health. If the charging voltage set point is high, it is a good indicator that the alternator is working hard to provide current to all systems and charging the battery to an SOC of 100%.

At the alternator connector (**FIGURE 20**), the L-terminal is the control circuit and the F-terminal is the field circuit. The field circuit is a feedback circuit that is used by the control module to monitor for performance and diagnostics.

FIGURE 20 Alternator connector.

NOTES

A pulse width modulation (PWM) signal is used for communication. Earlier systems used a 5 V PWM signal, and later systems use a 12 V PWM signal.

The PWM signal has a variable 128 Hz frequency. The frequency is not fixed; it will float slightly. An erratic, bouncing frequency or an extremely high frequency is usually related to interference. This will illuminate the battery warning light and set codes but will not affect charging system output (**FIGURE 21**).

FIGURE 21 Alternator.

Signal interference is usually related to wiring harness routing issues. Check to make sure the harness is not running close to the ignition coils. Also, check the technical service bulletin (TSB) for powertrain control module (PCM) reflashes.

TABLE 4 shows a list of on-board diagnostics (OBD) and diagnostic trouble codes (DTCs) associated with the charging system.

TABLE 4 OBD and DTCs

On-Board Diagnostics	Diagnostic Trouble Codes
System voltage fluctuation	P0560
System voltage unstable	P0561
System voltage low	P0562
System voltage high	P0563
Generator control circuit malfunction	P0620
Generator lamp "L" control circuit malfunction	P0621
Generator field "F" control circuit malfunction	P0622
Malfunction indicator lamp (MIL) control circuit	P0650

TECH TIP

DTCs P0620 and P0621 can commonly be found in the code history on the scan tool and are usually related to an intermittent connector issue at the alternator.

Intermittent wiring harness connections can cause the battery warning light to flicker. Check for loose connections or harness faults, particularly in the voltage regulator harness and plug (**FIGURE 22**).

To isolate a connector issue, graph the battery voltage, the L-terminal command, and the F-terminal signal PIDs (**FIGURE 23**). While monitoring the F-terminal, wiggle the alternator connector and look for dropouts or changes in the graphing pattern that indicate a connection problem.

FIGURE 22 Pigtail.

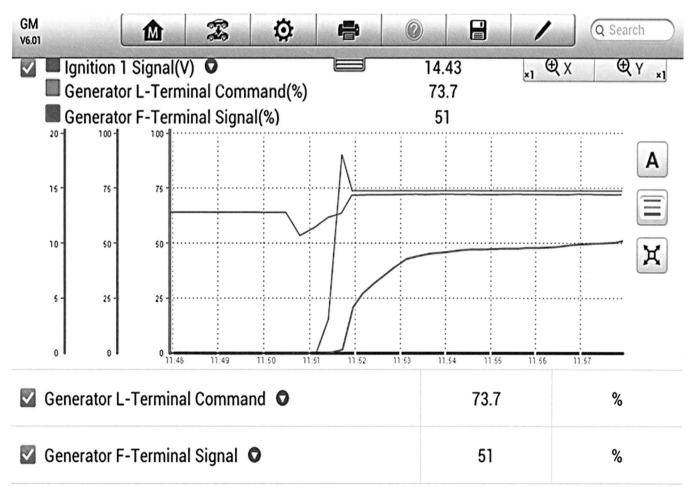

FIGURE 23 Graphed alternator PIDs.

If the PWM signal to the L-terminal should become open, the default charging rate is 13.8 V (**FIGURE 24**). With some systems, disconnection of the current sensor or generator battery control module (GBCM) will result in a default of 15.5 V.

FIGURE 24 Default voltage.

RVC Versions

There are two versions of the RVC charging system. The first is the stand-alone RVC (SARVC) and the other is the integrated RVC.

A key component of the SARVC system is the GBCM (**FIGURE 25**), which is basically a current clamp that surrounds the negative battery cable. When an electrical component is turned on, there is an instant increase in current flow. The more components that are operating, the greater the amperage required to supply those components. By measuring the current flow at the battery cable, the sensor continually monitors the system's total electrical demands so that charging voltage can be adjusted accordingly. The GBCM directly controls the duty cycle on the L-terminal (**FIGURE 26**).

FIGURE 25 Generator battery control module.

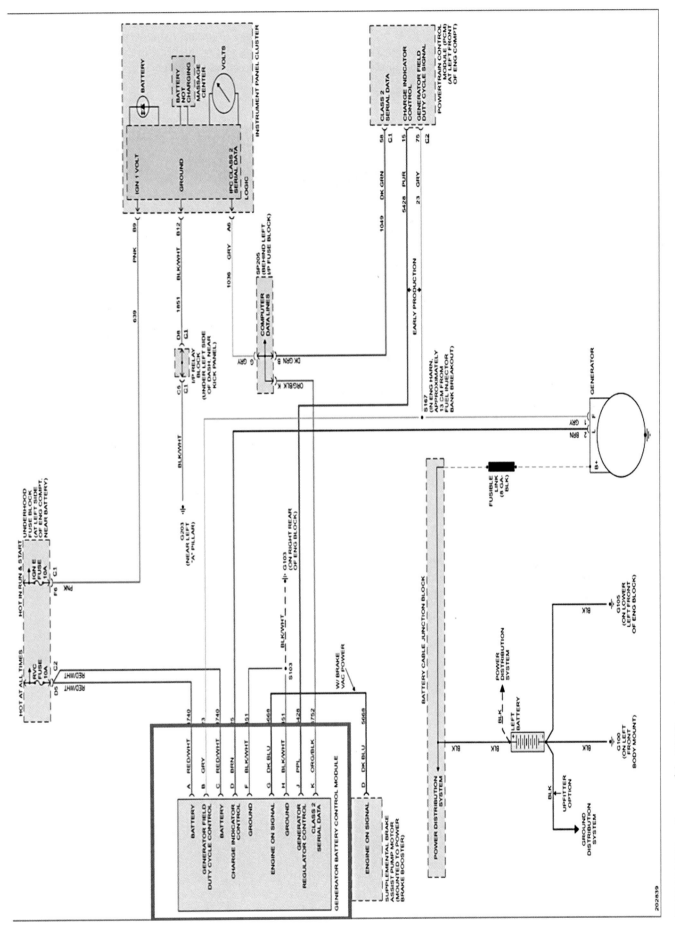

FIGURE 26 Wiring diagram of the SARVC system.

In the integrated RVC system (also known as the dual-module system), the body control module (BCM) receives battery current sensor (**FIGURE 27**) inputs and determines the required alternator output. This information is sent to the PCM over the GMLAN bus. The PCM controls the output of the alternator based on this input.

FIGURE 27 Current sensor.

FIGURE 28 shows a wiring diagram of the RVC system. The current sensor is much smaller. Depending on vehicle application, the sensor can surround either the positive or the negative battery cable.

When viewing current sensor data with a scan tool, positive readings indicate that the battery is charging. Negative readings indicate that the battery is discharging (**FIGURE 29**).

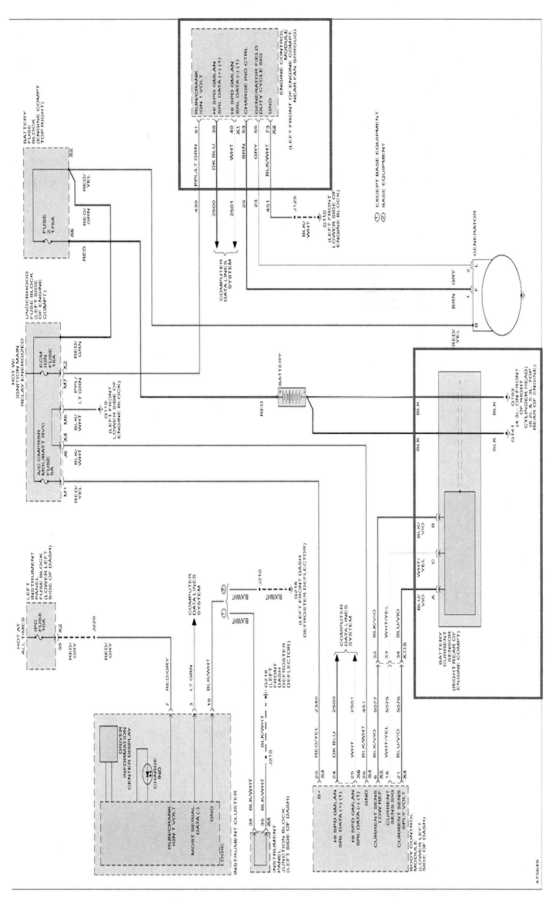

FIGURE 28 Wiring diagram of the integrated RVC system.

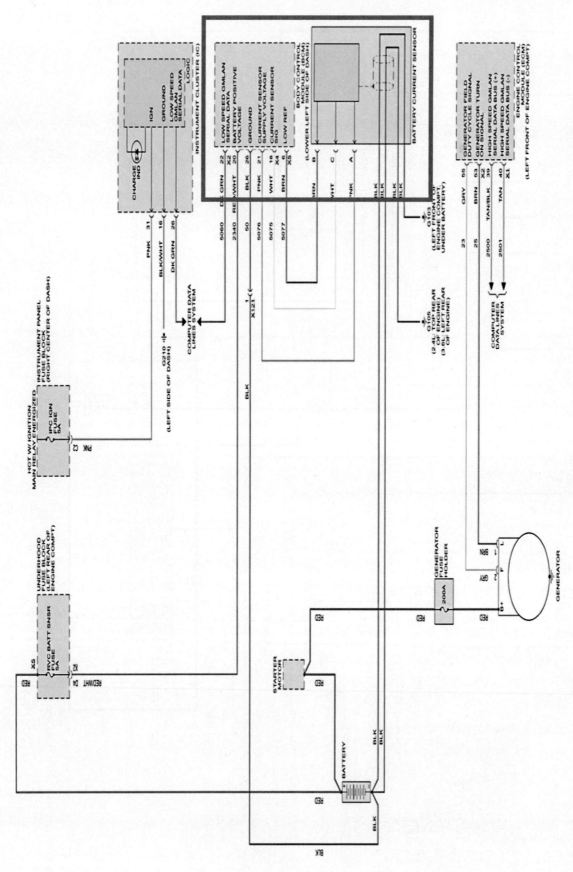

FIGURE 29 System diagram.

Load Shedding

The battery current sensor can also perform additional monitoring of the electrical system and status of the vehicle battery. If the current sensor detects charging system failure, or the vehicle battery condition is deteriorating, electrical load shedding actions are taken (**TABLE 5**). Load shedding reduces electrical power consumption by turning off nonessential electrical loads.

TABLE 5 Load Shedding Chart

Level	System	Action
0	None	None
1	Heated outside mirrors	"L" cycled at 80% duty cycle. Off 4 seconds out of every 20 seconds. Indicator not affected.
	Message center	No messages or indicators displayed. Data stored to indicate that Load Shed 1 was entered.
2	Heated outside mirrors, rear defroster, heated seats	"L" cycled at 50% duty cycle. Off 10 seconds out of every 20 seconds.
	Message center	"Battery Save Action" message displayed or flashing indicators.
3	Heated outside mirrors, rear defroster	System turned OFF. Indicators not affected.
	Message center	"Battery Saver Action" message displayed and/or "Battery/Charging System Failure" icon is illuminated. Chime is activated until Load Shed 3 is exited.

Load shedding may occur in stages depending on the SOC of the battery. The electrical loads that may be switched off include the following:

- Heated seats/vented seats/heated steering wheel
- Rear defroster and heated mirrors
- HVAC system
- 115 V AC power inverter system
- Audio and telematics system

TECH TIP

Between 2006 and 2009, load shedding levels could not be seen on a scan tool. Load shed information is included in the data stream on later applications.

When diagnosing load shedding issues, determine the conditions in which the load shedding occurs. Increase engine speed to between 2500 and 3000 RPM for about 60 seconds. If the system does not exit load shedding, there could be a programming issue that may be remedied by reprogramming the module.

RVC Modes of Operation

The RVC operates in different modes based on the inputs. The modes are displayed on the scan tool as being "Active" or "Inactive." Not all modes are used on all vehicles. The following are the different modes of operation:

- Charge mode
  - A software glitch causes the 2006 to 2008 Cobalt and Equinox to stick in this mode.
- Fuel economy mode
- Voltage reduction mode
- Battery sulfation mode
  - Extended operation in this mode can be caused by a low battery.
- Windshield deice mode
- Startup mode

Scan Tool Data

Monitor the actual battery voltage and desired battery voltage PIDs (**FIGURE 30**). The actual voltage should be close to the desired voltage (**FIGURE 31**).

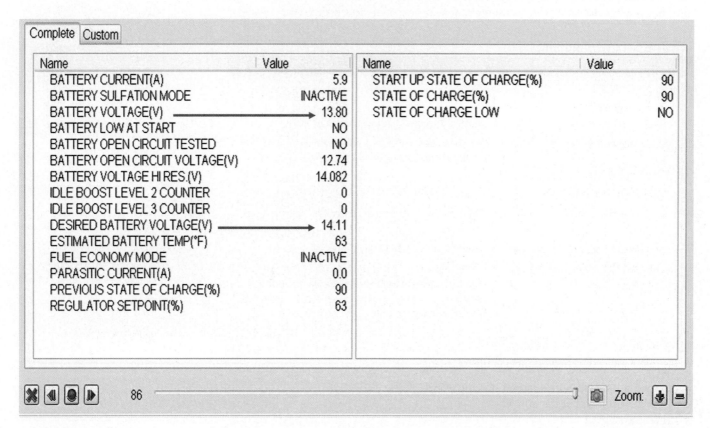

FIGURE 30 Electrical data.

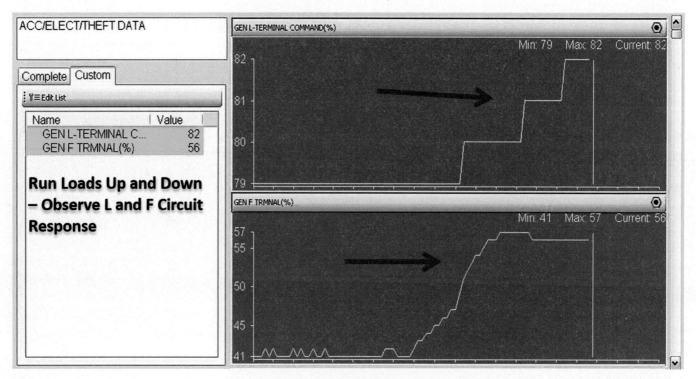

FIGURE 31 Graphing charging PIDs A.

Monitor the L and F circuit response as electrical loads are turned on and off (**FIGURE 32**).

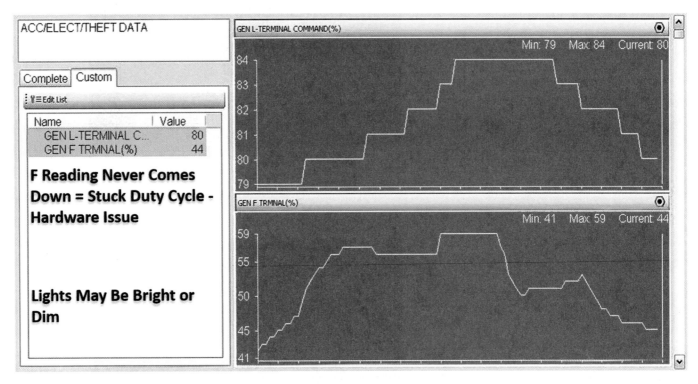

FIGURE 32 Graphing charging PIDs B.

Engine Control Module to Alternator Communication

To confirm that the commands of the engine control module (ECM) are being transmitted to the alternator, conduct the hardline test. This will require a properly equipped DVOM or a graphing multimeter. **FIGURES 33** to **42** show the different test connections.

A

FIGURE 33 Connect the meter to the battery ground terminal and the control side of the alternator circuit. **A.** Connection to the negative battery post.

NOTES

B

FIGURE 33 (*continued*). **B.** Connection to the alternator command circuit.

A

B

FIGURE 34 As electrical loads are applied, the duty cycle should increase. **A.** Duty cycle reading at idle, no loads. **B.** Duty cycle reading with loads applied.

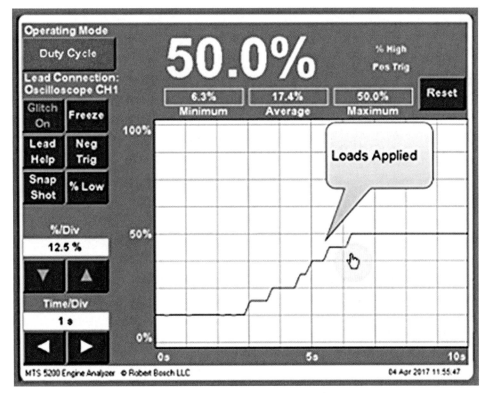

A

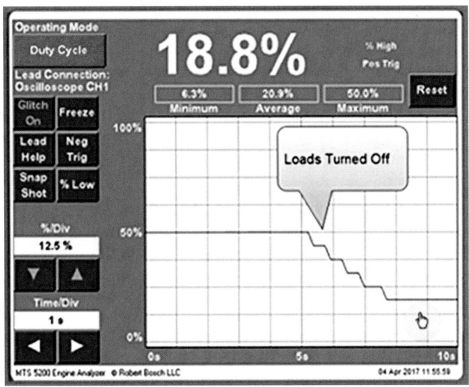

B

FIGURE 35 If the duty cycle commands are reaching the alternator but the alternator output is not changing, the alternator is faulty. **A.** Loads applied. **B.** Loads turned off.

NOTES

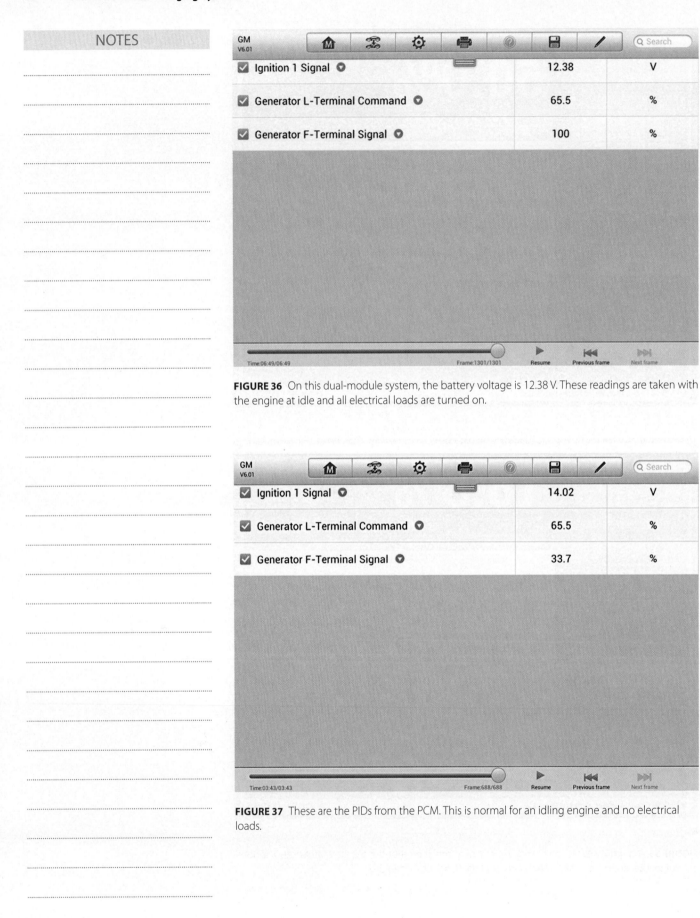

FIGURE 36 On this dual-module system, the battery voltage is 12.38 V. These readings are taken with the engine at idle and all electrical loads are turned on.

FIGURE 37 These are the PIDs from the PCM. This is normal for an idling engine and no electrical loads.

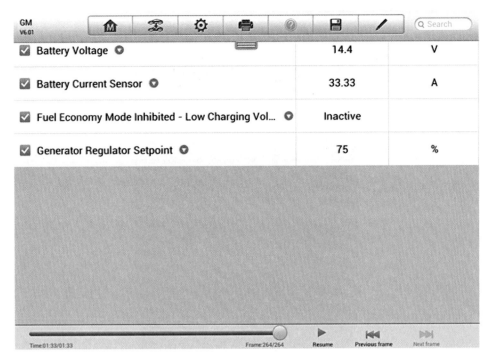

FIGURE 38 Here are the data PIDs from the BCM. Remember, in this system the BCM is the decision maker and the PCM is the driver. Note the battery voltage and the battery current sensor input. Positive readings indicate the amount of current going into the battery; negative readings indicate the amount leaving the battery.

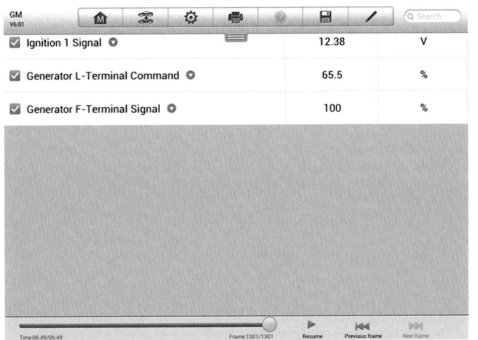

FIGURE 39 Going back to the original screenshot when the engine was at idle and all the electrical loads were activated—the voltage is below 12.6 V and the F-terminal is 100%, but the command is 65%. In this screenshot, the F-terminal is a substituted value. The true reading coming out of the alternator is 0%.

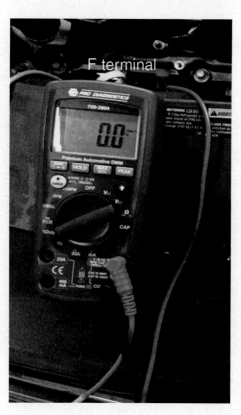

FIGURE 40 The command being 0% is confirmed by a DVOM.

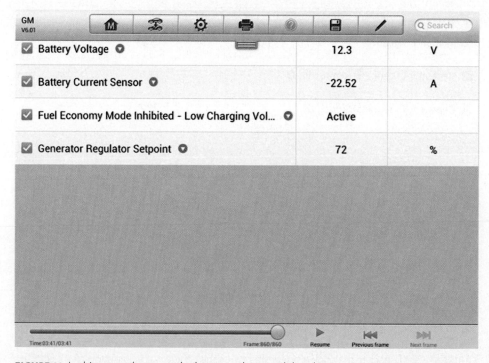

FIGURE 41 In this screenshot, note the battery voltage and that the current sensor reading is negative. The loads are being powered by the battery and the alternator is turned off. This is the mode for fuel economy (note that the fuel economy mode is active). This is the normal operation, but it could lead some technicians to think the alternator or system is not operating properly. This is an instance when alternator output does not increase with load.

NOTES

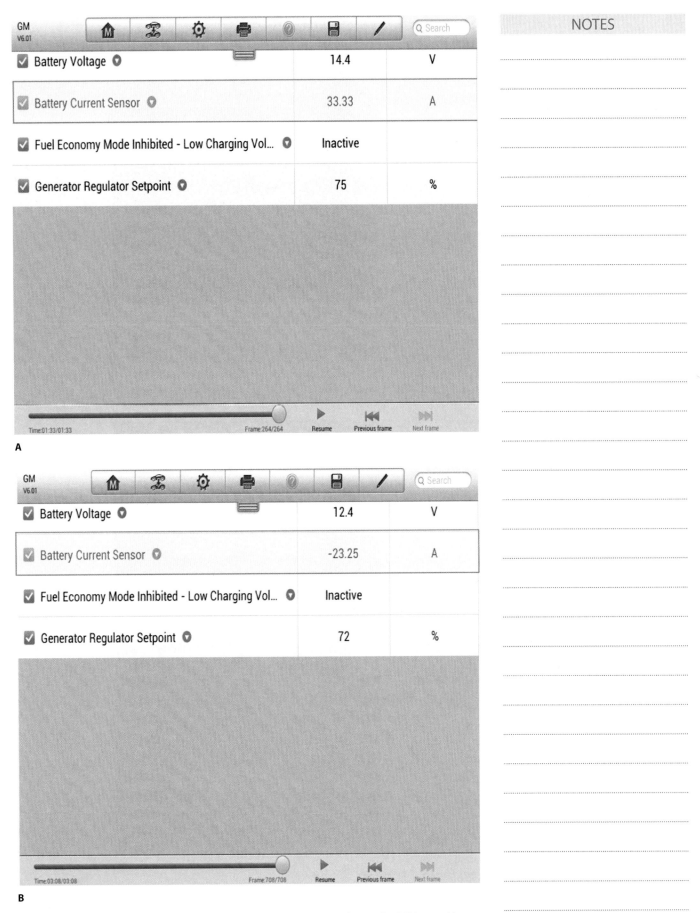

FIGURE 42 As mentioned, when observing the battery current sensor data at the BCM, a positive value **(A)** indicates that the battery is charging. If the value is negative **(B)**, the battery is discharging.

Duty Cycle Measurement—DVOM

To measure the duty cycle commands from the PCM to the alternator, first set the meter to the duty cycle function (**FIGURE 43**). Connect the positive meter lead to the "Command" or "Feedback" circuits at the alternator. Connect the negative test lead to the battery negative terminal.

FIGURE 43 DVOM duty cycle selection.

Changes in electrical loads should change the duty cycle commands at the alternator. Lower electrical loads should have a lower duty cycle command (**FIGURE 44A**). Higher electrical loads should have a higher duty cycle command (**FIGURE 44B**).

A

B

FIGURE 44 A. Lower electrical load with a low duty cycle command. **B.** Higher electrical load with a high duty cycle command.

Avoid pitfalls when using the DVOM to measure duty cycle. You must know your equipment and whether the circuit being tested is controlled by an HSD or LSD. Some meters provide a means of switching between positive and negative, some switch automatically, and some will not have a means of changing.

DVOMs that do not have a way to change the trigger (or if the trigger has not been changed by the user) will display inverse duty cycle readings. In this case, as electrical loads increase, the duty cycle decreases. This is due to some DVOMs monitoring the ground side of a digital signal. Therefore, with positive duty cycle, the ground side duty cycle reading increases with the alternator's "on" time.

Ford Charging Systems

Ford charging systems (**FIGURE 45**) use two circuits: control circuits and feedback circuits. The control circuit, called generator command (GENCOM) or generator regulator command (GENRC), is simply the command circuit and communicates the regulator set point.

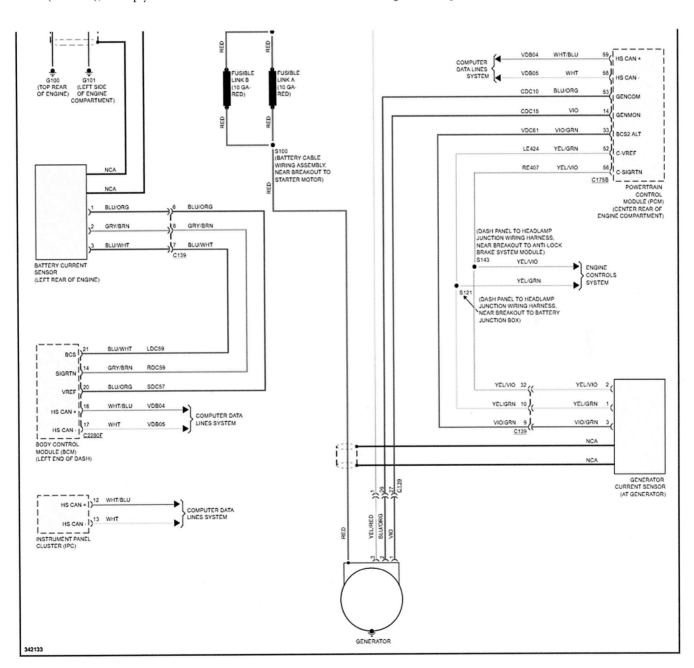

FIGURE 45 Wiring diagram—Ford.

The feedback circuit, called the generator monitor (GENMON) or the generator load input (GENLI), is used by the regulator to send feedback to the PCM in response to the communication signal (**FIGURE 46**).

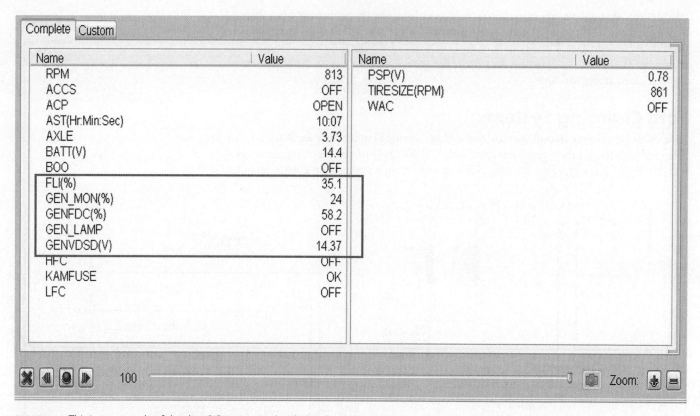

Complete	Custom			

Name	Value	Name	Value
RPM	813	PSP(V)	0.78
ACCS	OFF	TIRESIZE(RPM)	861
ACP	OPEN	WAC	OFF
AST(Hr:Min:Sec)	10:07		
AXLE	3.73		
BATT(V)	14.4		
BOO	OFF		
FLI(%)	35.1		
GEN_MON(%)	24		
GENFDC(%)	58.2		
GEN_LAMP	OFF		
GENVDSD(V)	14.37		
HFC	OFF		
KAMFUSE	OK		
LFC	OFF		

100   Zoom:

FIGURE 46 This is an example of the data PIDs associated with the charging system.

NOTES

Three wire charging systems (**FIGURE 47**) were used in Ford charging systems until the 2006 model year (MY). The third circuit is used to determine if the regulator is accurately maintaining the desired voltage set point.

FIGURE 47 Ford 3-wire connector.

Ford systems are notorious for fuse box corrosion (**FIGURE 48**), which can affect the operation of the charging system. A good method for detecting corrosion is to use a light-emitting diode (LED) flashlight. Corrosion is highly reflective when using an LED flashlight in a dark area. Shine the light into any open areas and look for blue or green sparkles that indicate corrosion.

FIGURE 48 Corroded fuse box.

An underhood fuse box is shown in **FIGURE 49**.

FIGURE 49 Ford underhood fuse box.

In most Ford applications, the electronic engine control (EEC) relay is the input for system voltage. This is displayed as "VPWR" (vehicle power) in the scan tool PID list.

Temperature Sensors

A faulty temperature sensor can cause charging system issues. When diagnosing issues with the charging system, if a temperature sensor DTC is present, address the temperature sensor fault first. For example, a low intake air temperature (IAT) reading can cause high alternator output. A high IAT reading can result in no alternator output.

NOTES

Dual Current Sensors

Late Ford models use dual current sensors. One is the battery current sensor and the other is the generator current sensor.

The battery current sensor (**FIGURE 50**) can be found around the ground cable from the battery terminal. This sensor is wired directly to the BCM.

FIGURE 50 Ford battery current sensor.

The generator current sensor (**FIGURE 51**) is typically located at the alternator B+ terminal. This sensor is wired directly to the PCM (**FIGURE 52**).

FIGURE 51 Ford generator current sensor.

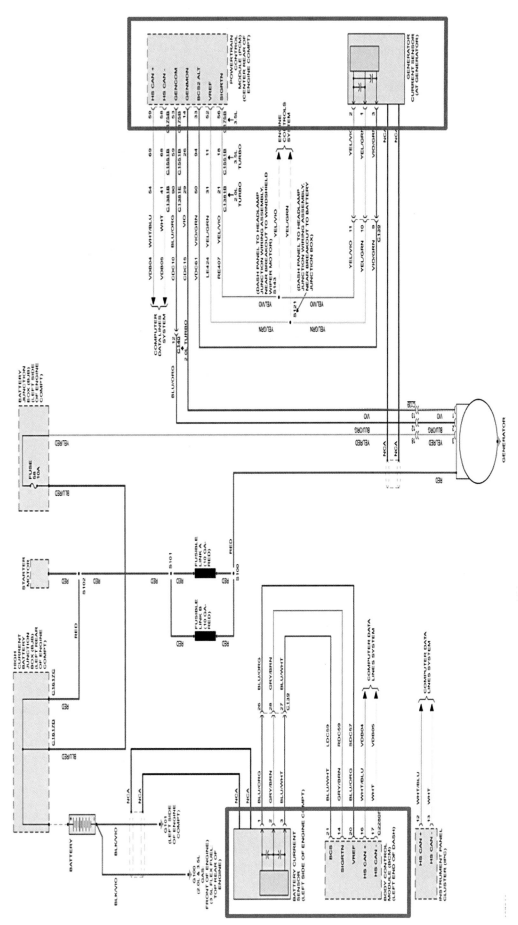

FIGURE 52 Ford wiring diagram—dual current sensors.

The 2.7L turbo engine has the generator current sensor on the negative post of the battery. This sensor can be confused with the battery current sensor (**FIGURE 53**) due to its location (**FIGURE 54**).

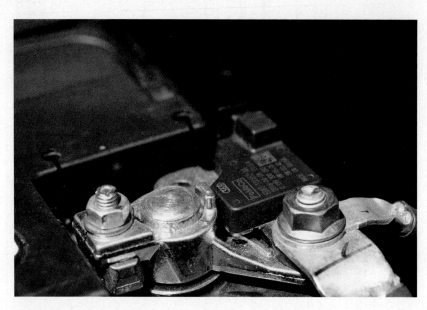

FIGURE 53 Ford smart battery sensor.

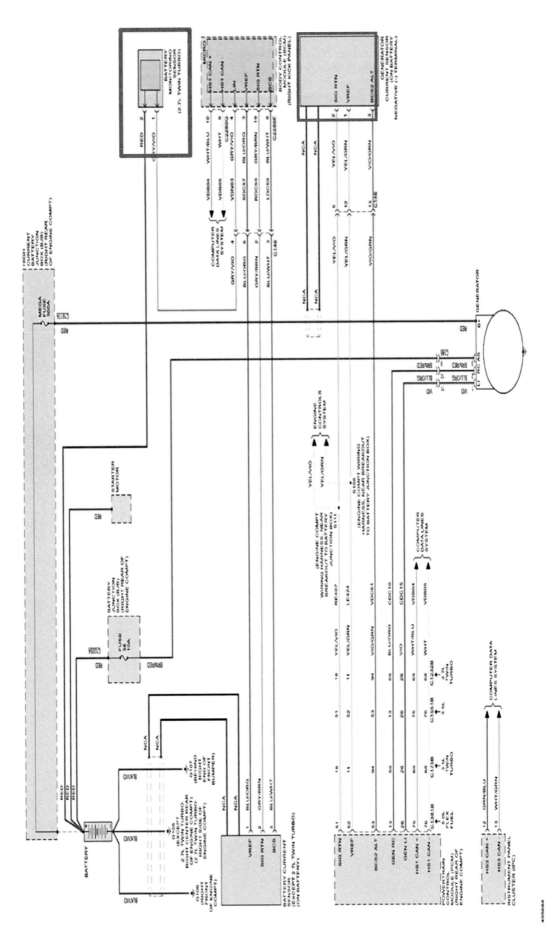

FIGURE 54 Ford wiring diagram—smart battery sensor (2.7L turbo).

Scan Tool Testing

Bidirectional control (**FIGURE 55**) allows the scan tool to command the generator by changing the voltage set point.

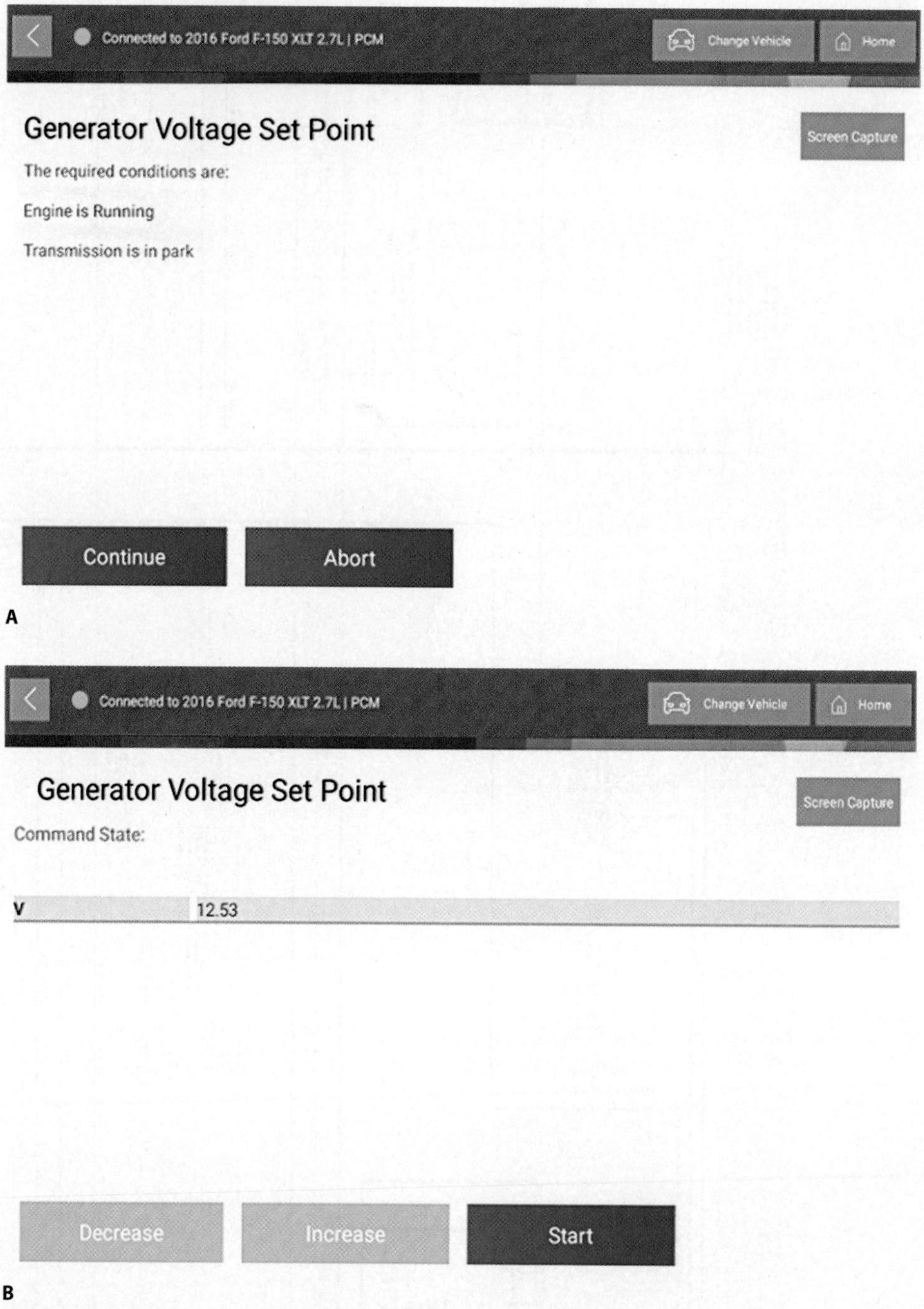

A

B

FIGURE 55 Bidirectional controls. **A.** Step 1. **B.** Step 2.

FIGURES 56 to **58** show some graphing examples of scan tool data PIDs.

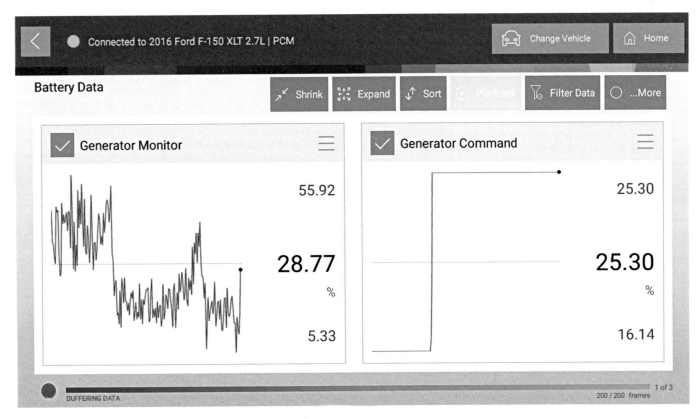

FIGURE 56 Graphing alternator PIDs—monitor and command.

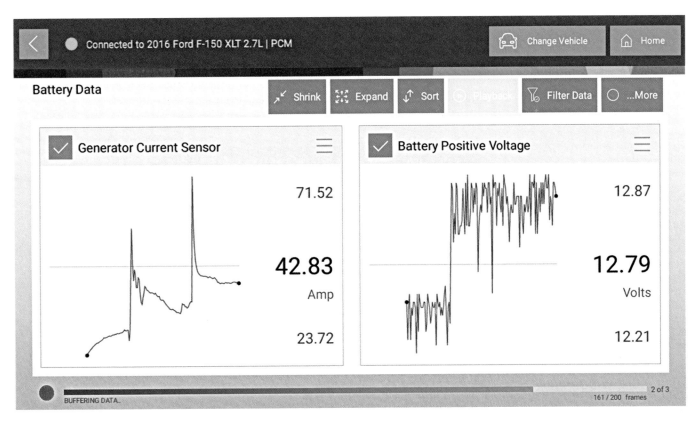

FIGURE 57 Graphing alternator current and battery voltage PIDs.

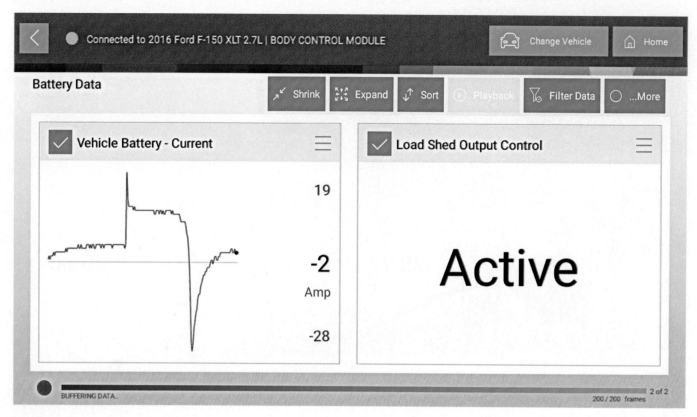

FIGURE 58 Battery data.

NOTES

Battery Registration

FIGURE 59 is a screenshot of the scan tool that identifies indicators that the system uses battery registration. Ford does have the capability to automatically register a battery after replacement. The system will automatically register the new battery if the vehicle has sat undisturbed for 12 hours. Obviously this is not ideal; it is always best to perform the registration immediately after battery replacement to ensure proper function.

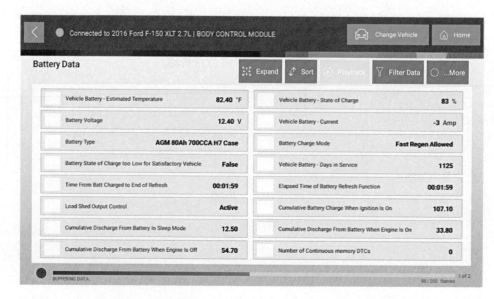

FIGURE 59 Charging PIDs in the BCM.

Ford PCM Harness Repair

The PCM terminals are very small and are susceptible to poor connection issues. Use drag pins or testers in the proper size to confirm that the terminal has not expanded (**FIGURE 60**).

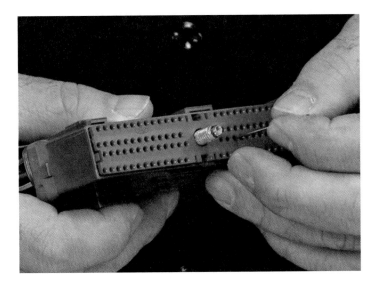

FIGURE 60 PCM connector.

TECH TIP

Wire gauge–sized drill bits can be used as an alternative to the drag pins.

Camshaft Position Sensor

The code DTC P0340 for the camshaft position (CMP) sensor (**FIGURE 61**) is common in Ford applications. It is estimated that 15% of CMP sensor codes are associated with alternator problems. A faulty alternator can cause excessive noise on the CMP sensor signal circuit.

A lab scope is one of the most reliable tools to use to see noise or glitches in the CMP sensor signal (**FIGURE 62**). A DVOM will not catch these events. The PCM only needs to see a 100 to 200 mV change from positive to negative crossing zero.

FIGURE 61 Camshaft sensor.

FIGURE 63 shows excessive noise on the CMP sensor signal circuit. Note that the voltage goes from positive to negative and crosses zero at several locations. This will cause the PCM to count the signals.

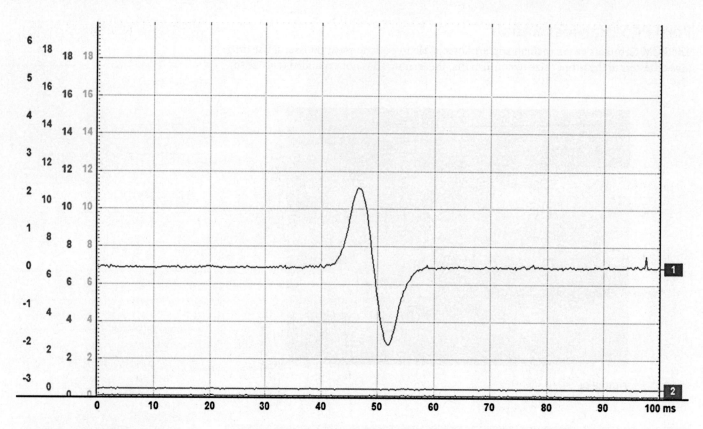

FIGURE 62 Camshaft sensor signal.

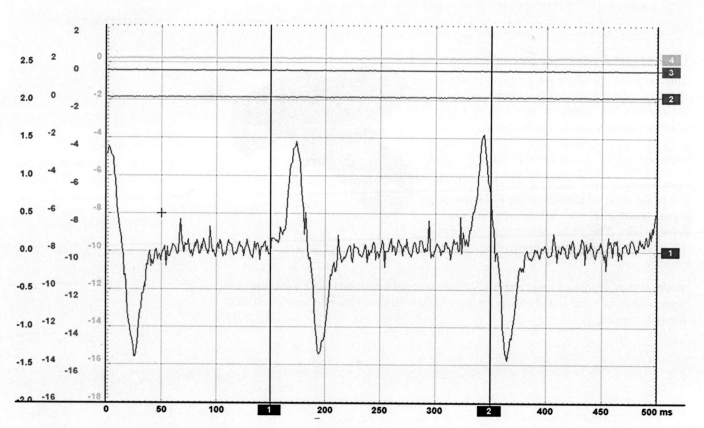

FIGURE 63 Cam sensor pattern with AC ripple.

Dual Alternator System

Ford Power Stroke diesels use various versions of the dual alternator system. **FIGURE 64** shows the dual alternator system on a 2007 6.0L Power Stroke.

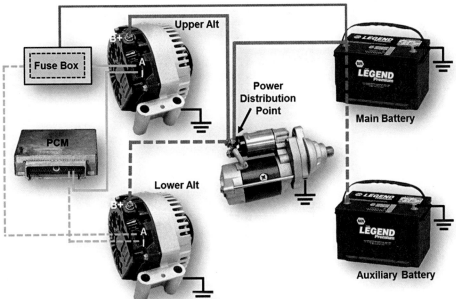

FIGURE 64 Dual alternator system on a 2007 6.0L Ford Power Stroke.

The upper alternator is rated at 140 amps. The lower alternator is rated at 120 amps. The two alternators are not interchangeable. Both alternators are independently controlled by individual internal voltage regulators.

The lower alternator is shut down by the PCM when the glow plugs are commanded on.

The alternator circuits are identified as the following:

- **B+** Alternator output to batteries and electrical system
- **I** Dual purpose:
  - PCM supplies voltage to turn on the regulator
  - Provides for alternator monitoring by the PCM
- **A** Supplies 13 to 15 V to the field coil
- **S** Turns on charging system warning light

It is important to verify that both the upper and the lower alternators are working. Upper alternator failures may occur because the lower alternator is not working properly. One possibility is that a failed glow plug timer is not allowing the lower alternator to turn on (**FIGURE 65**).

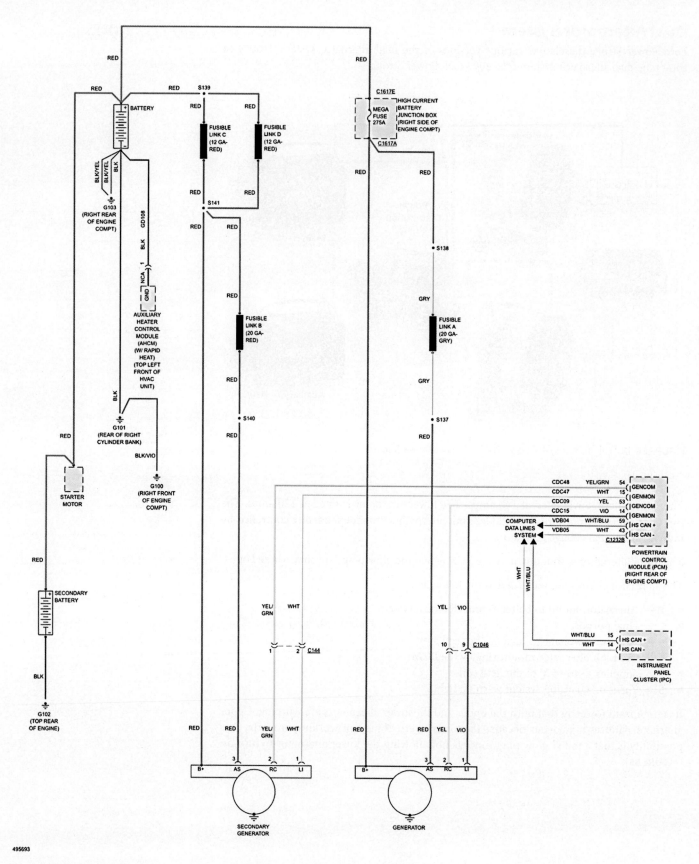

495693

FIGURE 65 Ford wiring diagram—dual alternator system.

The 6.7L Power Stroke (**FIGURE 66**) uses a smart charge system. The main alternator is rated at 200 amps and the secondary alternator is rated at 160 amps. The main and secondary alternators are not interchangeable. Both alternators are monitored and controlled by the PCM.

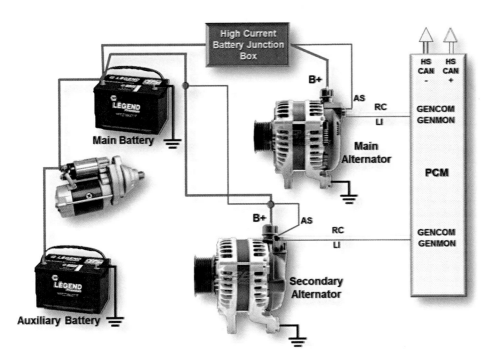

FIGURE 66 Ford 6.7L Power Stroke.

The PCM keeps the secondary alternator in a standby state where it does not generate until the main alternator reaches full output and additional current is needed. At this point, the secondary alternator kicks in.

The PCM controls the voltage regulator set point and duty cycle commands by the circuit between the GENCOM connection at the PCM and the alternator regulator control (RC) circuit. Duty cycle commands range from 3% to 98%. When monitoring the commands, it is important to note that if there are no set point changes needed, several seconds may elapse between command signals from the PCM to the regulator. Communication will appear as bursts of PWM signals.

The PCM does not allow alternator output until the engine is started and running. The PCM then slowly increases generator output to the required voltage. The PCM controls the warning indicator lamp by sending messages over the high-speed controller area network (HS CAN) bus to the instrument panel cluster (IPC) by way of the BCM.

The PCM uses vehicle speed sensor (VSS), engine coolant temperature (ECT), and other input information for charging system voltage control. Battery temperature is inferred using the IAT sensor.

During high current demands or low battery charge, the PCM raises engine speed as needed to increase alternator output (**FIGURE 67**).

If the GENCOM circuit fails to initiate charging, the generator may still be able to charge the battery and keep the engine running. If the engine momentarily operates at more than 2000 RPM, the generator will "self-excite" and enter default mode. Default mode produces approximately 13.5 V. The charge system warning lamp will illuminate, or the message center will display a "Check Charging System" message.

NOTES

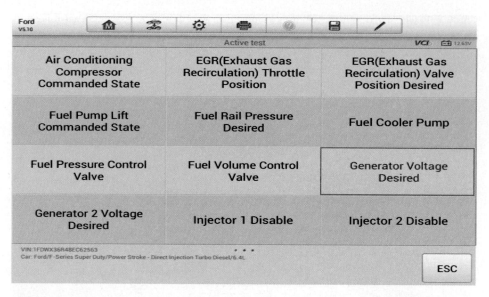

FIGURE 67 Bidirectional test.

The circuits of the Ford smart charge system include:

- **B+** Alternator output to the batteries and the vehicle electrical system
- **RC** Conducts duty cycle commands from the PCM's GENCOM circuit to the alternator's voltage regulator to control voltage output
- **LI** Provides feedback from the voltage regulator to the PCM by way of the GENMON circuit
- **AS** Dedicated to monitor or sense battery voltage

The scan tool may provide bidirectional controls for the charging system (**FIGURES 68** and **69**).

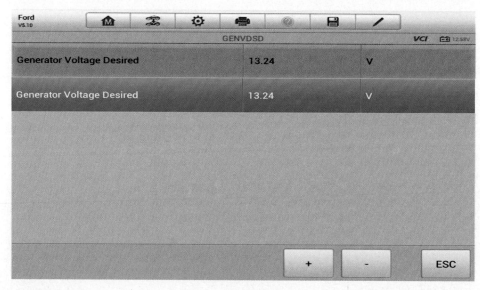

FIGURE 68 Some scan tools will allow you to select the voltage set point. While altering the set point, monitor the changes in commands and output.

☑ Generator Command ⊙	32.15	%
☑ Generator 2 Command ⊙	3.92	%
☑ Generator Fault Indicator Lamp ⊙	Off	
☑ Generator Monitor1 ⊙	68.75	%
☑ Generator 2 Monitor ⊙	0	%
☑ Generator Monitor Frequency ⊙	127	Hz
☑ Generator 2 Monitor Frequency ⊙	125	Hz
☑ Generator Voltage Desired ⊙	13.24	V
☑ Generator 2 Voltage Desired ⊙	6	V

Time:04:54/04:54 Frame:385/385 Resume Previous frame Next frame

FIGURE 69 This is an example of the data that may be available from some scan tools.

Chrysler Charging Systems

Chrysler has controlled the charge rate by using the PCM as the voltage regulator since the 1980s (**FIGURE 70**). The PCM uses PWM to regulate the field current. A goal voltage is determined from current battery voltage and battery temperature. The field current is turned on until the sensed voltage is about 0.5 V above the target goal voltage. At that time, it is turned off. The field current is turned on again once sensed voltage drops 0.5 V below the goal voltage.

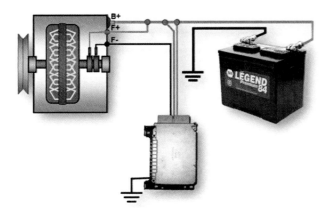

FIGURE 70 Chrysler system.

FIGURE 71 shows a single-board engine controller (SBEC), which uses an LSD to control the field circuit. Power to the field coil is supplied by the automatic shutdown (ASD) relay.

TECH TIP

If no power is supplied to the alternator, check the wiring from the ASD relay to the alternator. If the ASD is faulty, the vehicle will not start. Understanding how the system operates reduces diagnostic time.

FIGURE 71 Single-board engine controller.

FIGURE 72 shows a Jeep/Truck Engine Controller (JTEC), which supplies power to the alternator field coil. An LSD is used to control the ground side of the coil.

TECH TIP

The most common driver failure for the PCM is not supplying voltage to the alternator. If there is no voltage present at the alternator, perform a backprobe/pin test at the PCM. If there is voltage present at the connector, it's a wiring fault.

FIGURE 72 Jeep/Truck Engine Controller.

FIGURE 73 shows a next-generation controller (NGC) that supplies voltage and ground for the field circuit. Regulation is controlled by the ECM that pulse width modulates an HSD the voltage to the field.

FIGURE 73 Next-generation controller.

Any problems with the field circuit, including an open rotor or worn-out brushes in the alternator, will be reported as a DTC. Over- and undercharging conditions that do not meet "target" or "goal" voltage by 1 V will also set a DTC.

TECH TIP

Similar to the JTEC, except that it is a positive duty cycle, the voltage in an NGC is pulsed and the ground stays constant.

Battery Temperature Sensor/Ambient Air Temperature Sensor

Battery temperature is the major input used to determine the goal voltage of the charging system. Most newer Chrysler vehicles use a dedicated battery temperature sensor (BTS) that is located at the bottom of the battery tray and contacts the battery case (**FIGURE 74**). If a BTS is not used, the battery temperature is inferred from the ambient air temperature (AAT) sensor.

FIGURE 74 Chrysler battery temperature sensor.

NOTES

When monitoring the scan tool data, confirm that the BTS input is accurate. A faulty input can result in the overcharging or undercharging of the battery.

TECH TIP

If the spring breaks on the BTS, the sensor will relax into the cavity of the battery tray. This creates a gap and can affect the accuracy of the battery temperature reading, which will affect the alternator output.

Diagnosing the Charging System

The diagnostic process begins with checking for DTCs. If DTCs are set, it will lead to proper circuit tests. While standard on-board diagnostics second-generation (OBD-II) charging system fault codes list the nature of a charging system problem, they often do not isolate the actual cause of the problem. Manual testing is required to determine the cause. In addition, aftermarket scan tools or code readers may not have access to all fault code information. Manufacturers may also use 1600 series manufacturer-specific codes along with the standard OBD-II-related codes. Reading of these manufacturer-specific codes may not be available using generic scan tools. Once again, manually testing procedures like those we are discussing can be employed to isolate the cause of a charging system problem.

Field Control Checks

Begin by testing for battery voltage at both alternator terminals during key on/engine off (KOEO). There should be voltage at both terminals.

If no voltage is present at either terminal, check the ASD relay or PCM power supply. If there is voltage at only one terminal, there is an open circuit in the alternator.

With both terminals still backprobed at the alternator (**FIGURE 75**), set the DVOM (or lab scope) to read the duty cycle. Start the engine and allow it to idle. Observe the duty cycle as electrical loads are added. It is helpful to have a second DVOM connected across the battery to read charging voltage.

FIGURE 75 Backprobe connector.

If the duty cycle changes, this means that the PCM recognizes a load and is attempting to correct it. If there is no charge voltage at the battery but a duty cycle is present, then this is most likely an alternator fault. However, if the duty cycle never changes or the DVOM shows no reading, then this is a circuit fault or PCM fault.

Overcharge

Electronic voltage output control uses a sense circuit to monitor the battery voltage. Based on this input, the alternator is activated and deactivated to maintain the proper battery voltage. If there is a drop in voltage on the sense circuit, the PCM will increase the charge rate.

Resistance on the sense circuit can result in the battery overcharging. For example, if the target voltage is 14.3 V and the voltage sense circuit has a 2 V drop due to resistance, actual charge output at the alternator will be 16.3 V. The PCM thinks there is nothing wrong, but system voltage is higher than normal by the amount of the unwanted voltage drop. In systems that use an external voltage sense circuit, this can be an overlooked cause of overcharging. Replacing the alternator will not fix the problem.

The scan tool only reports what the PCM is seeing. Use a DVOM to compare actual battery voltage with the voltage data PID (**FIGURE 76**). Believe the DVOM. If there is a difference in the readings, check the voltage sense circuit for resistance. Also, check the battery terminals for tightness and corrosion. In addition, check the PCM ground circuits for excessive resistance.

TECH TIP

This can also be used to quickly test for power and ground issues for communication faults. Most communication faults are caused by poor connection, power, and ground integrity. With the DVOM hooked to the battery, scan data from each module and read voltage PID (which is on every module's data list), then compare readings. They should be within 0.2 V of each other.

FIGURE 76 Scanner/DVOM comparison.

CASE STUDY

Chrysler PT Cruiser

The owner of a 2010 PT Cruiser (FIGURE 77) purchased the vehicle from a "Buy Here, Pay Here" dealership. The dealership claimed the vehicle was reconditioned. However, the owner has had to replace the battery 4 times in 9 months of ownership.

The following summarizes the service history of the vehicle:

FIGURE 77   2010 PT Cruiser.

- Trip 1: The technician pushed the vehicle into the shop. The battery was so dead that it would not even power up the tester. The battery was replaced, and a full system test was performed—all passed.
- Trip 2: Two months later, same result. The technician replaced the battery and performed a full system test. All tests passed. The technician also checked for DTCs—none were recorded. The vehicle was kept for 2 days to check for key-off drains—none were found.
- Trip 3: Three months later, same thing. Battery was replaced, full system test was run with two different testers—all passed. The technician sent the vehicle to the dealer, who spent 5 days with it and could not duplicate the problem.
- Trip 4: Two months later, same thing. Now the dealer buys the car back. The battery is replaced again.

In this type of situation, begin by ignoring that system tests were performed in the past. You want to run your own diagnostics and make your own determinations. In this scenario, the system tests did pass again. There were no DTCs recorded. This is not surprising because the battery was completely drained.

FIGURE 78 shows the scan tool data PIDs for the charging system. When monitoring the scan tool data, battery voltage and goal voltage should be within 0.5 V. This means the alternator is doing exactly what the PCM is commanding. As electrical loads are turned on, the readings should follow each other.

Complete	Custom			
⋮ ▼ ≡ Edit List				
Name	Value		Name	Value
Engine Speed(RPM)	712			
Target Charging Voltage(V)	13.711			
Voltage Sense(V)	13.911			
Battery Volt(V)	13.834			

FIGURE 78   Scan tool data PIDs for the charging system.

Chrysler Intelligent Battery Sensor Charging System

Some Chrysler vehicles use input from the intelligent battery sensor (IBS) (**FIGURE 79**) and other sensors to maintain and charge battery voltage. The accelerator pedal position (APP), manifold absolute pressure (MAP), and vehicle speed inputs are also used.

FIGURE 79 Chrysler intelligent battery sensor.

The IBS communicates with the BCM over the LIN bus. The BCM then relays the information to the PCM on the controller area network (CAN) bus.

During engine cruise and acceleration, the charging system (**FIGURE 80**) delivers enough voltage to allow battery stabilization. During deceleration, the charging system will output maximum regulated voltage in order to replenish the battery.

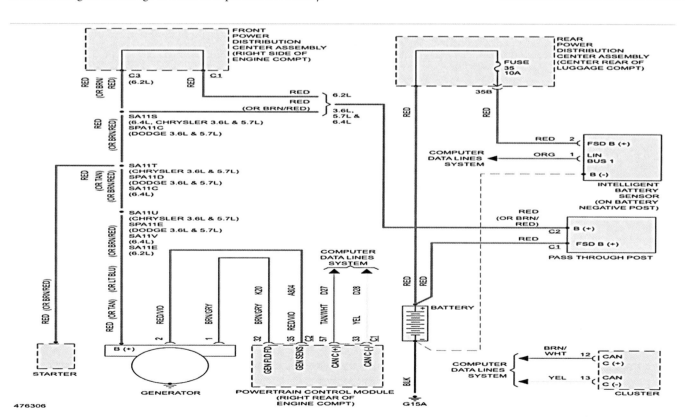

FIGURE 80 Chrysler charging system wiring diagram.

The PCM regulates the output of the charging system by PWM of the HSD circuit to the field winding. The PCM receives a voltage input from the generator and from the power distribution center (PDC). These voltage levels are compared to the desired voltage levels programmed in the software.

The 2-terminal and the B+ terminal are internally connected to provide a voltage reading to the PCM on the sense circuit. The internal connection allows for the B+ voltage to be monitored. If the B+ terminal stud is loose or disconnected, the PCM will shut down the generator field.

TABLE 6 lists PIDs in LIN smart battery sensors.

TABLE 6 2017 Chrysler 300 5.7L V8 MPI

IBS Lifetime Charge Received (AmpHrs)	1,319.625
IBS Lifetime Charge Released (AmpHrs)	1,252.250
IBS Measured Voltage (V)	14.3505859
IBS Predicted Time Limit for Start Capability (Min)	336
IBS Predicted Voltage after Cranking (V)	10.6250
IBS Response Error	No
IBS SOC (%)	83
IBS State of Health (AmpHrs)	79.5
IBS Temperature (°F)	75
IBS Temperature Error	No Error
IBS Voltage before LIN Wakeup (V)	12.77

FIGURE 81 shows LIN smart battery sensor communication via scope waveform.

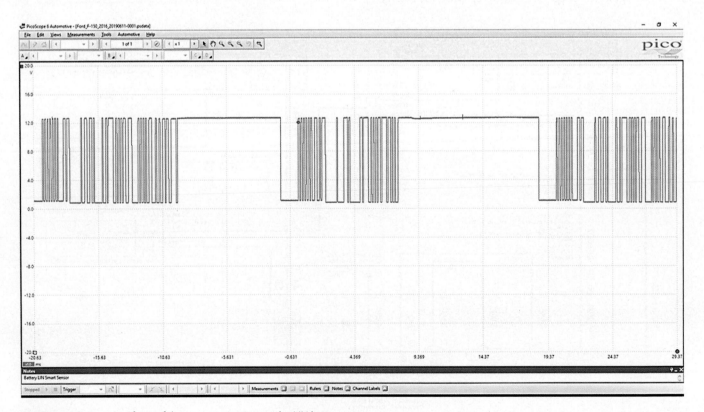

FIGURE 81 Scope waveform of the communication on the LIN bus.

Load Reduction

In cases where the IBS detects a charging system failure or the vehicle battery conditions are deteriorating, electrical load reduction actions will take place to extend the driving time and distance of the vehicle. This is done by turning off or reducing power to nonessential electrical loads. The electrical loads that may be switched off (if equipped) and vehicle functions that can be affected by load reduction include the following:

- Heated seats/vented seats/heated wheel
- Heated/cooled cupholders
- Rear defroster and heated mirrors
- HVAC system
- 115 V AC power inverter system
- Audio and telematics systems

Load reduction takes place only while the engine is running. A message will be displayed to the driver if there is a failure or depletion detected. "Battery Saver" or "Battery Save Mode" will appear in the message center.

LIN Bus Alternators

Many of today's vehicles use network-controlled charging systems. Most manufacturers use the LIN bus for this function.

Some manufacturers use an interfaced generator that communicates with the PCM via the LIN bus. The LIN interface allows the PCM to control the generator to supply power on demand. The generator houses a newly designed voltage regulator that controls generator output voltage. The voltage regulator contains integrated electronics with driver stages and a microprocessor.

The PCM sends voltage set point data to the generator. In turn, the voltage regulator sends data to the PCM concerning generator load and field excitation current. To protect the generator, the excitation current is limited based on engine speed.

On computer-controlled charging systems that do not use an interfaced generator, the PCM uses the IBS to determine required alternator output to meet the demand and controls the activation of the field winding. The PCM regulates the output of the charging system by PWM of the HSD circuit to the field winding.

Diagnostic Resources

No Alternator Voltage Output Test

If the base voltage is higher than the charging voltage, there is no alternator output (**FIGURE 82**). This does not automatically condemn the alternator.

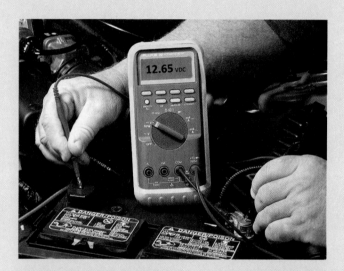

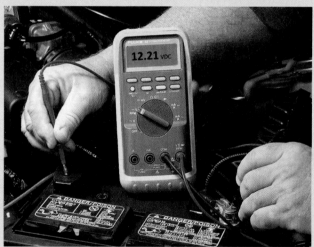

FIGURE 82 Base voltage higher than charging voltage.

The purpose of the no voltage output test is to determine whether the lack of voltage output is due to a fault in the B+ harness circuit. To perform this test, follow these steps:

1. Turn the ignition off.
2. Set the DVOM to the DC volts scale.
3. Place the positive meter lead on the alternator B+ terminal.
4. Place the negative meter lead on the alternator case.
5. The reading should be at—or very near—battery voltage.

If the reading shows no—or very low—voltage, look for a broken B+ harness wire, bad connection, or burned fusible link. Also make sure that the alternator is properly grounded. If the reading shows at or very near battery voltage, proceed to the regulator harness test.

Regulator Harness Test

The purpose of the regulator harness test is to determine whether the no voltage output condition is due to a fault in the regulator harness circuit. Voltage from the regulator circuit is used as a "turn on" signal to the alternator. Without this voltage, the alternator will not operate. To perform this test, follow these steps:

1. Disconnect the voltage regulator harness from the regulator plug.
2. Probe the positive test lead of the DVOM for voltage at the appropriate harness terminal (**FIGURE 83**). This will vary according to vehicle application and model, so it will be necessary to refer to a vehicle schematic to find the test location.
3. Connect the negative meter lead to the negative post of the battery.
4. Turn the ignition to the RUN position, but do not start the engine.

FIGURE 83 Performing the regulator harness test.

No voltage at the terminal can be caused by an open harness wire, a burned-out dash warning light, or a computer issue.

If there is voltage at the appropriate harness pin and the voltage is good at the B+ harness, replace the alternator.

Excessive Voltage Output Test

When the engine is running, if the voltage reading at the battery exceeds 16 V, turn the engine off and conduct the following test before condemning the alternator or voltage regulator (**FIGURE 84**).

FIGURE 84 Excessive voltage output test.

The purpose of this test is to determine whether excessive alternator voltage output is due to a fault in the sensing circuit. To perform this test, follow these steps:

1. Set the DVOM to the DC volts scale.
2. Turn the ignition off.
3. Disconnect the voltage regulator harness from the regulator plug.
4. Turn the ignition to the RUN position, but do not start the engine.
5. Attach the negative meter lead to a suitable grounding point.
6. Check for battery voltage at the sense terminal in the harness with positive DVOM test lead.

The reading at the sense terminal should be within 0.1 V of battery voltage. If the voltage is correct on an internally regulated alternator, replace the alternator. If the alternator uses an external voltage regulator, make sure the external regulator is properly grounded. If it is, the regulator is bad and needs to be replaced.

If the voltage reading at the sense terminal is low, there is excessive resistance in the circuit that must be located and repaired; otherwise, the internal or external voltage regulator will attempt to adjust the alternator voltage output according to the low reading. This will cause excessive alternator voltage output from an otherwise good alternator.

Parasitic Drain Test

The purpose of the parasitic drain test is to determine how much drain is occurring when the engine and all the vehicle electrical loads are turned off. There are two methods for performing the test: the amp clamp method and the ammeter method (**FIGURE 85**).

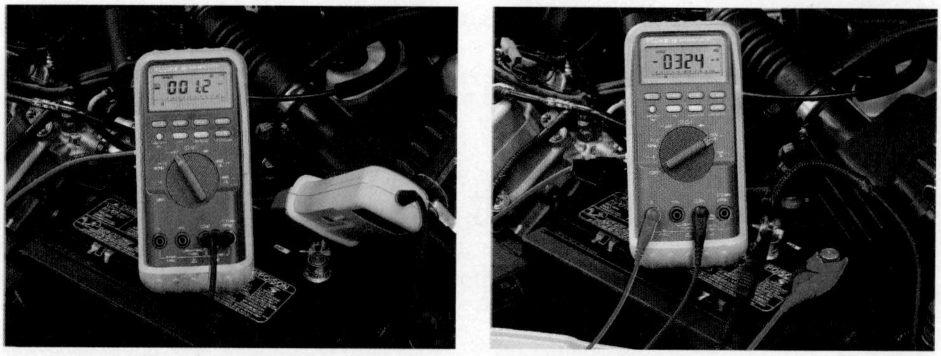

A   B

FIGURE 85 Parasitic drain test. **A.** Using an amp clamp. **B.** Using an ammeter.

Determine which method to use by considering how quickly the battery is draining. If a battery is draining within a few hours, the amp clamp method is the best choice. If it takes a few days for the battery to discharge, the ammeter method will provide the most accurate testing results.

To use the ammeter to perform the parasitic drain test, follow these steps:

1. Place the ignition in the OFF position and turn off all vehicle electrical accessories. Make sure that all glove box, trunk, and underhood lights are off.
2. Let the vehicle sit for 40 to 60 minutes with everything turned off so that the computers and other electronic components can time out and go into sleep modes. Failing to do this will produce inaccurately high parasitic drain readings.
3. Connect the keep-alive battery.
4. Set the DVOM to the DC volts scale. Connect the negative meter lead to the common input and the positive test lead to the amperage input that best corresponds to the expected amperage reading.
5. Based on ease of access, disconnect either the positive or the negative battery cable.
6. Connect one of the meter leads to the disconnected battery cable and the other lead to the battery post. Observe polarity when making the test lead connections.
7. Disconnect the keep-alive battery.
8. Observe the reading on the meter.

Results

For most vehicles, any reading that exceeds 100 mA is excessive. A 175 mA parasitic drain can discharge most batteries within a few days. A 2 amp parasitic drain can discharge most batteries within a few hours.

If the reading shows an excessive parasitic drain, the cause of the excessive drain must be located and corrected.

Old Test Method—Pulling Fuses

In the past, searching for drains was performed by pulling fuses and watching for drops in meter readings (**FIGURE 86**). Pulling fuses in late model vehicles may actually reactivate sleeping circuits and cause meter readings to increase.

FIGURE 86 Pulling fuses to test for drains.

Fuse Voltage Drop Test
Procedure
Set a DVOM to the millivolt scale and check for voltage drops across the fuses, as shown in **FIGURE 87**.

FIGURE 87 Checking for voltage drop across fuses using a DVOM.

Any significant millivolt reading across a fuse indicates that current is flowing in that circuit. If a fuse reading shows a significant voltage drop, find out what is staying on in that circuit to see whether it is causing the excessive drain. Fuse voltage drop values can be found in **TABLES 8** through **11**.

TECH TIP

After completing the test and locating the cause of an excessive drain, be sure to reconnect the keep-alive battery before disconnecting the ammeter from the battery and cable. After reconnecting the cable to the battery, disconnect the keep-alive battery from the vehicle.

TABLE 8 Mini Fuse Voltage Drop Chart—Circuit Current across Fuse

Fuse Voltage Drop Chart - Mini Fuse
Circuit Current Across Fuse (milliAmps)

Fuse Color	Grey	Violet	Pink	Tan	Brown	Red	Blue	Yellow	Clear	Green
Measurement mV	Mini 2 Amp	Mini 3 Amp	Mini 4 Amp	Mini 5 Amp	Mini 7.5 Amp	Mini 10 Amp	Mini 15 Amp	Mini 20 Amp	Mini 25 Amp	Mini 30 Amp
0.1	2	3	4	6	9	13	22	31	42	54
0.2	4	6	9	11	18	27	44	62	85	108
0.3	5	9	13	17	28	40	66	93	127	162
0.4	7	12	17	23	37	54	87	125	169	216
0.5	9	15	21	28	46	67	109	156	212	270
0.6	11	18	26	34	55	81	131	187	254	324
0.7	13	21	30	39	65	94	153	218	297	378
0.8	14	24	34	45	74	108	175	249	339	432
0.9	16	27	38	51	83	121	197	280	381	486
1	18	30	43	56	92	135	218	312	424	541
1.1	20	33	47	62	101	148	240	343	466	595
1.2	22	36	51	68	111	162	262	374	508	649
1.3	23	39	55	73	120	175	284	405	551	703
1.4	25	41	60	79	129	189	306	436	593	757
1.5	27	44	64	85	138	202	328	467	636	811
1.6	29	47	68	90	147	216	349	498	678	865
1.7	31	50	72	96	157	229	371	530	720	919
1.8	32	53	77	101	166	243	393	561	763	973
1.9	34	56	81	107	175	256	415	592	805	1027
2	36	59	85	113	184	270	437	623	847	1081
2.1	38	62	89	118	194	283	459	654	890	1135
2.2	40	65	94	124	203	296	480	685	932	1189
2.3	41	68	98	130	212	310	502	717	975	1243
2.4	43	71	102	135	221	323	524	748	1017	1297
2.5	45	74	106	141	230	337	546	779	1059	1351
2.6	47	77	111	146	240	350	568	810	1102	1405
2.7	49	80	115	152	249	364	590	841	1144	1459
2.8	50	83	119	158	258	377	611	872	1186	1514
2.9	52	86	124	163	267	391	633	903	1229	1568
3	54	89	128	169	276	404	655	935	1271	1622
3.1	56	92	132	175	286	418	677	966	1314	1676
3.2	58	95	136	180	295	431	699	997	1356	1730
3.3	59	98	141	186	304	445	721	1028	1398	1784
3.4	61	101	145	192	313	458	742	1059	1441	1838
3.5	63	104	149	197	323	472	764	1090	1483	1892
3.6	65	107	153	203	332	485	786	1121	1525	1946
3.7	67	110	158	208	341	499	808	1153	1568	2000
3.8	68	113	162	214	350	512	830	1184	1610	2054
3.9	70	116	166	220	359	526	852	1215	1653	2108
4	72	119	170	225	369	539	873	1246	1695	2162
4.1	74	121	175	231	378	553	895	1277	1737	2216
4.2	76	124	179	237	387	566	917	1308	1780	2270
4.3	77	127	183	242	396	580	939	1340	1822	2324
4.4	79	130	187	248	406	593	961	1371	1864	2378
4.5	81	133	192	254	415	606	983	1402	1907	2432
4.6	83	136	196	259	424	620	1004	1433	1949	2486
4.7	85	139	200	265	433	633	1026	1464	1992	2541
4.8	86	142	204	270	442	647	1048	1495	2034	2595
4.9	88	145	209	276	452	660	1070	1526	2076	2649
5	90	148	213	282	461	674	1092	1558	2119	2703

TABLE 8 Mini Fuse Voltage Drop Chart—Circuit Current across Fuse *(continued)*

Fuse Voltage Drop Chart - Mini Fuse
Circuit Current Across Fuse (milliAmps)

Fuse Color	Grey	Violet	Pink	Tan	Brown	Red	Blue	Yellow	Clear	Green
Measurement mV	Mini 2 Amp	Mini 3 Amp	Mini 4 Amp	Mini 5 Amp	Mini 7.5 Amp	Mini 10 Amp	Mini 15 Amp	Mini 20 Amp	Mini 25 Amp	Mini 30 Amp
5.1	92	151	217	287	470	687	1114	1589	2161	2757
5.2	94	154	221	293	479	701	1135	1620	2203	2811
5.3	95	157	226	299	488	714	1157	1651	2246	2865
5.4	97	160	230	304	498	728	1179	1682	2288	2919
5.5	99	163	234	310	507	741	1201	1713	2331	2973
5.6	101	166	239	315	516	755	1223	1745	2373	3027
5.7	103	169	243	321	525	768	1245	1776	2415	3081
5.8	104	172	247	327	535	782	1266	1807	2458	3135
5.9	106	175	251	332	544	795	1288	1838	2500	3189
6	108	178	256	338	553	809	1310	1869	2542	3243
6.1	110	181	260	344	562	822	1332	1900	2585	3297
6.2	112	184	264	349	571	836	1354	1931	2627	3351
6.3	113	187	268	355	581	849	1376	1963	2669	3405
6.4	115	190	273	361	590	863	1397	1994	2712	3459
6.5	117	193	277	366	599	876	1419	2025	2754	3514
6.6	119	196	281	372	608	889	1441	2056	2797	3568
6.7	121	199	285	377	618	903	1463	2087	2839	3622
6.8	122	201	290	383	627	916	1485	2118	2881	3676
6.9	124	204	294	389	636	930	1507	2150	2924	3730
7	126	207	298	394	645	943	1528	2181	2966	3784
7.1	128	210	302	400	654	957	1550	2212	3008	3838
7.2	129	213	307	406	664	970	1572	2243	3051	3892
7.3	131	216	311	411	673	984	1594	2274	3093	3946
7.4	133	219	315	417	682	997	1616	2305	3136	4000
7.5	135	222	319	423	691	1011	1638	2336	3178	4054
7.6	137	225	324	428	700	1024	1659	2368	3220	4108
7.7	138	228	328	434	710	1038	1681	2399	3263	4162
7.8	140	231	332	439	719	1051	1703	2430	3305	4216
7.9	142	234	336	445	728	1065	1725	2461	3347	4270
8	144	237	341	451	737	1078	1747	2492	3390	4324
8.1	146	240	345	456	747	1092	1769	2523	3432	4378
8.2	147	243	349	462	756	1105	1790	2555	3475	4432
8.3	149	246	353	468	765	1119	1812	2586	3517	4486
8.4	151	249	358	473	774	1132	1834	2617	3559	4541
8.5	153	252	362	479	783	1146	1856	2648	3602	4595
8.6	155	255	366	485	793	1159	1878	2679	3644	4649
8.7	156	258	371	490	802	1173	1900	2710	3686	4703
8.8	158	261	375	496	811	1186	1921	2741	3729	4757
8.9	160	264	379	501	820	1199	1943	2773	3771	4811
9	162	267	383	507	829	1213	1965	2804	3814	4865
9.1	164	270	388	513	839	1226	1987	2835	3856	4919
9.2	165	273	392	518	848	1240	2009	2866	3898	4973
9.3	167	276	396	524	857	1253	2031	2897	3941	5027
9.4	169	279	400	530	866	1267	2052	2928	3983	5081
9.5	171	281	405	535	876	1280	2074	2960	4025	5135
9.6	173	284	409	541	885	1294	2096	2991	4068	5189
9.7	174	287	413	546	894	1307	2118	3022	4110	5243
9.8	176	290	417	552	903	1321	2140	3053	4153	5297
9.9	178	293	422	558	912	1334	2162	3084	4195	5351
10	180	296	426	563	922	1348	2183	3115	4237	5405

TABLE 9   Standard Fuse Voltage Drop Chart (ATO, ATC)—Circuit Current across Fuse (milliamps)

Fuse Voltage Drop Chart - Standard Fuse (ATO,ATC)

Circuit Current Across Fuse (milliAmps)

Fuse Color	Black	Grey	Violet	Pink	Tan	Brown	Red	Blue	Yellow	Clear	Green	Blu-Green	Orange
Measurement mV	Standard 1 Amp	Standard 2 Amp	Standard 3 Amp	Standard 4 Amp	Standard 5 Amp	Standard 7.5 Amp	Standard 10 Amp	Standard 15 Amp	Standard 20 Amp	Standard 25 Amp	Standard 30 Amp	Standard 35 Amp	Standard 40 Amp
0.1	1	2	3	4	6	9	13	21	30	40	51	62	69
0.2	2	4	6	9	11	18	26	42	59	79	102	124	139
0.3	2	6	10	13	17	27	39	63	89	119	152	186	208
0.4	3	7	13	18	22	37	52	83	118	159	203	248	278
0.5	4	9	16	22	28	46	65	104	148	198	254	311	347
0.6	5	11	19	26	34	55	78	125	178	238	305	373	417
0.7	6	13	23	31	39	64	91	146	207	278	355	435	486
0.8	7	15	26	35	45	73	104	167	237	317	406	497	556
0.9	7	17	29	39	50	82	117	188	266	357	457	559	625
1	8	19	32	44	56	92	130	208	296	397	508	621	694
1.1	9	21	35	48	62	101	143	229	325	437	558	683	764
1.2	10	22	39	53	67	110	156	250	355	476	609	745	833
1.3	11	24	42	57	73	119	169	271	385	516	660	807	903
1.4	11	26	45	61	78	128	182	292	414	556	711	870	972
1.5	12	28	48	66	84	137	195	313	444	595	761	932	1042
1.6	13	30	51	70	90	147	208	333	473	635	812	994	1111
1.7	14	32	55	75	95	156	221	354	503	675	863	1056	1181
1.8	15	34	58	79	101	165	234	375	533	714	914	1118	1250
1.9	15	36	61	83	106	174	247	396	562	754	964	1180	1319
2	16	37	64	88	112	183	260	417	592	794	1015	1242	1389
2.1	17	39	68	92	118	192	273	438	621	833	1066	1304	1458
2.2	18	41	71	96	123	202	286	458	651	873	1117	1366	1528
2.3	19	43	74	101	129	211	299	479	680	913	1168	1429	1597
2.4	20	45	77	105	134	220	312	500	710	952	1218	1491	1667
2.5	20	47	80	110	140	229	325	521	740	992	1269	1553	1736
2.6	21	49	84	114	146	238	338	542	769	1032	1320	1615	1806
2.7	22	50	87	118	151	247	351	563	799	1071	1371	1677	1875
2.8	23	52	90	123	157	257	364	583	828	1111	1421	1739	1944
2.9	24	54	93	127	162	266	377	604	858	1151	1472	1801	2014
3	24	56	96	132	168	275	390	625	888	1190	1523	1863	2083
3.1	25	58	100	136	174	284	403	646	917	1230	1574	1925	2153
3.2	26	60	103	140	179	293	416	667	947	1270	1624	1988	2222
3.3	27	62	106	145	185	302	429	688	976	1310	1675	2050	2292
3.4	28	64	109	149	190	312	442	708	1006	1349	1726	2112	2361
3.5	28	65	113	154	196	321	455	729	1036	1389	1777	2174	2431
3.6	29	67	116	158	202	330	468	750	1065	1429	1827	2236	2500
3.7	30	69	119	162	207	339	481	771	1095	1468	1878	2298	2569
3.8	31	71	122	167	213	348	494	792	1124	1508	1929	2360	2639
3.9	32	73	125	171	218	357	506	813	1154	1548	1980	2422	2708
4	33	75	129	175	224	367	519	833	1183	1587	2030	2484	2778
4.1	33	77	132	180	230	376	532	854	1213	1627	2081	2547	2847
4.2	34	79	135	184	235	385	545	875	1243	1667	2132	2609	2917
4.3	35	80	138	189	241	394	558	896	1272	1706	2183	2671	2986
4.4	36	82	141	193	246	403	571	917	1302	1746	2234	2733	3056
4.5	37	84	145	197	252	412	584	938	1331	1786	2284	2795	3125
4.6	37	86	148	202	258	422	597	958	1361	1825	2335	2857	3194
4.7	38	88	151	206	263	431	610	979	1391	1865	2386	2919	3264
4.8	39	90	154	211	269	440	623	1000	1420	1905	2437	2981	3333
4.9	40	92	158	215	275	449	636	1021	1450	1944	2487	3043	3403
5	41	93	161	219	280	458	649	1042	1479	1984	2538	3106	3472
5.1	41	95	164	224	286	467	662	1063	1509	2024	2589	3168	3542
5.2	42	97	167	228	291	477	675	1083	1538	2063	2640	3230	3611
5.3	43	99	170	232	297	486	688	1104	1568	2103	2690	3292	3681
5.4	44	101	174	237	303	495	701	1125	1598	2143	2741	3354	3750
5.5	45	103	177	241	308	504	714	1146	1627	2183	2792	3416	3819
5.6	46	105	180	246	314	513	727	1167	1657	2222	2843	3478	3889
5.7	46	107	183	250	319	522	740	1188	1686	2262	2893	3540	3958
5.8	47	108	186	254	325	532	753	1208	1716	2302	2944	3602	4028
5.9	48	110	190	259	331	541	766	1229	1746	2341	2995	3665	4097
6	49	112	193	263	336	550	779	1250	1775	2381	3046	3727	4167
6.1	50	114	196	268	342	559	792	1271	1805	2421	3096	3789	4236
6.2	50	116	199	272	347	568	805	1292	1834	2460	3147	3851	4306
6.3	51	118	203	276	353	577	818	1313	1864	2500	3198	3913	4375
6.4	52	120	206	281	359	587	831	1333	1893	2540	3249	3975	4444

TABLE 9 Standard Fuse Voltage Drop Chart (ATO, ATC)—Circuit Current across Fuse (milliamps) *(continued)*

Fuse Voltage Drop Chart - Standard Fuse (ATO,ATC)

Circuit Current Across Fuse (milliAmps)

Fuse Color	Black	Grey	Violet	Pink	Tan	Brown	Red	Blue	Yellow	Clear	Green	Blu-Green	Orange
Measurement mV	Standard 1 Amp	Standard 2 Amp	Standard 3 Amp	Standard 4 Amp	Standard 5 Amp	Standard 7.5 Amp	Standard 10 Amp	Standard 15 Amp	Standard 20 Amp	Standard 25 Amp	Standard 30 Amp	Standard 35 Amp	Standard 40 Amp
6.5	53	121	209	285	364	596	844	1354	1923	2579	3299	4037	4514
6.6	54	123	212	289	370	605	857	1375	1953	2619	3350	4099	4583
6.7	54	125	215	294	375	614	870	1396	1982	2659	3401	4161	4653
6.8	55	127	219	298	381	623	883	1417	2012	2698	3452	4224	4722
6.9	56	129	222	303	387	632	896	1438	2041	2738	3503	4286	4792
7	57	131	225	307	392	642	909	1458	2071	2778	3553	4348	4861
7.1	58	133	228	311	398	651	922	1479	2101	2817	3604	4410	4931
7.2	59	135	232	316	403	660	935	1500	2130	2857	3655	4472	5000
7.3	59	136	235	320	409	669	948	1521	2160	2897	3706	4534	5069
7.4	60	138	238	325	415	678	961	1542	2189	2937	3756	4596	5139
7.5	61	140	241	329	420	687	974	1563	2219	2976	3807	4658	5208
7.6	62	142	244	333	426	697	987	1583	2249	3016	3858	4720	5278
7.7	63	144	248	338	431	706	1000	1604	2278	3056	3909	4783	5347
7.8	63	146	251	342	437	715	1013	1625	2308	3095	3959	4845	5417
7.9	64	148	254	346	443	724	1026	1646	2337	3135	4010	4907	5486
8	65	150	257	351	448	733	1039	1667	2367	3175	4061	4969	5556
8.1	66	151	260	355	454	742	1052	1688	2396	3214	4112	5031	5625
8.2	67	153	264	360	459	752	1065	1708	2426	3254	4162	5093	5694
8.3	67	155	267	364	465	761	1078	1729	2456	3294	4213	5155	5764
8.4	68	157	270	368	471	770	1091	1750	2485	3333	4264	5217	5833
8.5	69	159	273	373	476	779	1104	1771	2515	3373	4315	5280	5903
8.6	70	161	277	377	482	788	1117	1792	2544	3413	4365	5342	5972
8.7	71	163	280	382	487	797	1130	1813	2574	3452	4416	5404	6042
8.8	72	164	283	386	493	807	1143	1833	2604	3492	4467	5466	6111
8.9	72	166	286	390	499	816	1156	1854	2633	3532	4518	5528	6181
9	73	168	289	395	504	825	1169	1875	2663	3571	4569	5590	6250
9.1	74	170	293	399	510	834	1182	1896	2692	3611	4619	5652	6319
9.2	75	172	296	404	515	843	1195	1917	2722	3651	4670	5714	6389
9.3	76	174	299	408	521	852	1208	1938	2751	3690	4721	5776	6458
9.4	76	176	302	412	527	862	1221	1958	2781	3730	4772	5839	6528
9.5	77	178	305	417	532	871	1234	1979	2811	3770	4822	5901	6597
9.6	78	179	309	421	538	880	1247	2000	2840	3810	4873	5963	6667
9.7	79	181	312	425	543	889	1260	2021	2870	3849	4924	6025	6736
9.8	80	183	315	430	549	898	1273	2042	2899	3889	4975	6087	6806
9.9	80	185	318	434	555	907	1286	2063	2929	3929	5025	6149	6875
10	81	187	322	439	560	917	1299	2083	2959	3968	5076	6211	6944

TABLE 10 Fuse Voltage Drop Chart—JCase Cartridge Style

Circuit Current Across Fuse (milliAmps)

Fuse Color	Blue	Pink	Green	Red	Yellow	Black	Blue
Measurement mV	Cartridge 20 Amp	Cartridge 30 Amp	Cartridge 40 Amp	Cartridge 50 Amp	Cartridge 60 Amp	Cartridge 80 Amp	Cartridge 100 Amp
0.1	17	19	26	42	59	81	213
0.2	33	38	53	83	118	163	426
0.3	50	58	79	125	176	244	638
0.4	67	77	105	167	235	325	851
0.5	83	96	132	208	294	407	1064
0.6	100	115	158	250	353	488	1277
0.7	117	135	184	292	412	569	1489
0.8	133	154	211	333	471	650	1702
0.9	150	173	237	375	529	732	1915
1	167	192	263	417	588	813	2128
1.1	183	212	289	458	647	894	2340
1.2	200	231	316	500	706	976	2553
1.3	217	250	342	542	765	1057	2766
1.4	233	269	368	583	824	1138	2979
1.5	250	288	395	625	882	1220	3191
1.6	267	308	421	667	941	1301	3404
1.7	283	327	447	708	1000	1382	3617
1.8	300	346	474	750	1059	1463	3830
1.9	317	365	500	792	1118	1545	4043
2	333	385	526	833	1176	1626	4255
2.1	350	404	553	875	1235	1707	4468
2.2	367	423	579	917	1294	1789	4681
2.3	383	442	605	958	1353	1870	4894
2.4	400	462	632	1000	1412	1951	5106
2.5	417	481	658	1042	1471	2033	5319
2.6	433	500	684	1083	1529	2114	5532
2.7	450	519	711	1125	1588	2195	5745
2.8	467	538	737	1167	1647	2276	5957
2.9	483	558	763	1208	1706	2358	6170
3	500	577	789	1250	1765	2439	6383
3.1	517	596	816	1292	1824	2520	6596
3.2	533	615	842	1333	1882	2602	6809
3.3	550	635	868	1375	1941	2683	7021
3.4	567	654	895	1417	2000	2764	7234
3.5	583	673	921	1458	2059	2846	7447
3.6	600	692	947	1500	2118	2927	7660
3.7	617	712	974	1542	2176	3008	7872
3.8	633	731	1000	1583	2235	3089	8085
3.9	650	750	1026	1625	2294	3171	8298
4	667	769	1053	1667	2353	3252	8511
4.1	683	788	1079	1708	2412	3333	8723
4.2	700	808	1105	1750	2471	3415	8936
4.3	717	827	1132	1792	2529	3496	9149
4.4	733	846	1158	1833	2588	3577	9362
4.5	750	865	1184	1875	2647	3659	9574
4.6	767	885	1211	1917	2706	3740	9787
4.7	783	904	1237	1958	2765	3821	10000
4.8	800	923	1263	2000	2824	3902	10213
4.9	817	942	1289	2042	2882	3984	10426
5	833	962	1316	2083	2941	4065	10638

TABLE 10 Fuse Voltage Drop Chart—JCase Cartridge Style *(continued)*

Circuit Current Across Fuse (milliAmps)

Fuse Color	Blue	Pink	Green	Red	Yellow	Black	Blue
Measurement mV	Cartridge 20 Amp	Cartridge 30 Amp	Cartridge 40 Amp	Cartridge 50 Amp	Cartridge 60 Amp	Cartridge 80 Amp	Cartridge 100 Amp
5.1	850	981	1342	2125	3000	4146	10851
5.2	867	1000	1368	2167	3059	4228	11064
5.3	883	1019	1395	2208	3118	4309	11277
5.4	900	1038	1421	2250	3176	4390	11489
5.5	917	1058	1447	2292	3235	4472	11702
5.6	933	1077	1474	2333	3294	4553	11915
5.7	950	1096	1500	2375	3353	4634	12128
5.8	967	1115	1526	2417	3412	4715	12340
5.9	983	1135	1553	2458	3471	4797	12553
6	1000	1154	1579	2500	3529	4878	12766
6.1	1017	1173	1605	2542	3588	4959	12979
6.2	1033	1192	1632	2583	3647	5041	13191
6.3	1050	1212	1658	2625	3706	5122	13404
6.4	1067	1231	1684	2667	3765	5203	13617
6.5	1083	1250	1711	2708	3824	5285	13830
6.6	1100	1269	1737	2750	3882	5366	14043
6.7	1117	1288	1763	2792	3941	5447	14255
6.8	1133	1308	1789	2833	4000	5528	14468
6.9	1150	1327	1816	2875	4059	5610	14681
7	1167	1346	1842	2917	4118	5691	14894
7.1	1183	1365	1868	2958	4176	5772	15106
7.2	1200	1385	1895	3000	4235	5854	15319
7.3	1217	1404	1921	3042	4294	5935	15532
7.4	1233	1423	1947	3083	4353	6016	15745
7.5	1250	1442	1974	3125	4412	6098	15957
7.6	1267	1462	2000	3167	4471	6179	16170
7.7	1283	1481	2026	3208	4529	6260	16383
7.8	1300	1500	2053	3250	4588	6341	16596
7.9	1317	1519	2079	3292	4647	6423	16809
8	1333	1538	2105	3333	4706	6504	17021
8.1	1350	1558	2132	3375	4765	6585	17234
8.2	1367	1577	2158	3417	4824	6667	17447
8.3	1383	1596	2184	3458	4882	6748	17660
8.4	1400	1615	2211	3500	4941	6829	17872
8.5	1417	1635	2237	3542	5000	6911	18085
8.6	1433	1654	2263	3583	5059	6992	18298
8.7	1450	1673	2289	3625	5118	7073	18511
8.8	1467	1692	2316	3667	5176	7154	18723
8.9	1483	1712	2342	3708	5235	7236	18936
9	1500	1731	2368	3750	5294	7317	19149
9.1	1517	1750	2395	3792	5353	7398	19362
9.2	1533	1769	2421	3833	5412	7480	19574
9.3	1550	1788	2447	3875	5471	7561	19787
9.4	1567	1808	2474	3917	5529	7642	20000
9.5	1583	1827	2500	3958	5588	7724	20213
9.6	1600	1846	2526	4000	5647	7805	20426
9.7	1617	1865	2553	4042	5706	7886	20638
9.8	1633	1885	2579	4083	5765	7967	20851
9.9	1650	1904	2605	4125	5824	8049	21064
10	1667	1923	2632	4167	5882	8130	21277

TABLE 11 Fuse Voltage Drop Chart—Maxi Fuse

Fuse Voltage Drop Chart - Maxi Fuse
Circuit Current Across Fuse (milliAmps)

Fuse Color	Yellow	Grey	Green	Blu-Green	Orange	Red	Blue	Tan	Clear
Measurement mV	Maxi 20 Amp	Maxi 25 Amp	Maxi 30 Amp	Maxi 35 Amp	Maxi 40 Amp	Maxi 50 Amp	Maxi 60 Amp	Maxi 70 Amp	Maxi 80 Amp
0.1	32	42	51	58	70	91	112	156	185
0.2	65	84	103	117	141	182	225	313	370
0.3	97	126	154	175	211	273	337	469	556
0.4	129	167	205	234	282	364	449	625	741
0.5	161	209	256	292	352	455	562	781	926
0.6	194	251	308	351	423	545	674	938	1111
0.7	226	293	359	409	493	636	787	1094	1296
0.8	258	335	410	468	563	727	899	1250	1481
0.9	290	377	462	526	634	818	1011	1406	1667
1	323	418	513	585	704	909	1124	1563	1852
1.1	355	460	564	643	775	1000	1236	1719	2037
1.2	387	502	615	702	845	1091	1348	1875	2222
1.3	419	544	667	760	915	1182	1461	2031	2407
1.4	452	586	718	819	986	1273	1573	2188	2593
1.5	484	628	769	877	1056	1364	1685	2344	2778
1.6	516	669	821	936	1127	1455	1798	2500	2963
1.7	548	711	872	994	1197	1545	1910	2656	3148
1.8	581	753	923	1053	1268	1636	2022	2813	3333
1.9	613	795	974	1111	1338	1727	2135	2969	3519
2	645	837	1026	1170	1408	1818	2247	3125	3704
2.1	677	879	1077	1228	1479	1909	2360	3281	3889
2.2	710	921	1128	1287	1549	2000	2472	3438	4074
2.3	742	962	1179	1345	1620	2091	2584	3594	4259
2.4	774	1004	1231	1404	1690	2182	2697	3750	4444
2.5	806	1046	1282	1462	1761	2273	2809	3906	4630
2.6	839	1088	1333	1520	1831	2364	2921	4063	4815
2.7	871	1130	1385	1579	1901	2455	3034	4219	5000
2.8	903	1172	1436	1637	1972	2545	3146	4375	5185
2.9	935	1213	1487	1696	2042	2636	3258	4531	5370
3	968	1255	1538	1754	2113	2727	3371	4688	5556
3.1	1000	1297	1590	1813	2183	2818	3483	4844	5741
3.2	1032	1339	1641	1871	2254	2909	3596	5000	5926
3.3	1065	1381	1692	1930	2324	3000	3708	5156	6111
3.4	1097	1423	1744	1988	2394	3091	3820	5313	6296
3.5	1129	1464	1795	2047	2465	3182	3933	5469	6481
3.6	1161	1506	1846	2105	2535	3273	4045	5625	6667
3.7	1194	1548	1897	2164	2606	3364	4157	5781	6852
3.8	1226	1590	1949	2222	2676	3455	4270	5938	7037
3.9	1258	1632	2000	2281	2746	3545	4382	6094	7222
4	1290	1674	2051	2339	2817	3636	4494	6250	7407
4.1	1323	1715	2103	2398	2887	3727	4607	6406	7593
4.2	1355	1757	2154	2456	2958	3818	4719	6563	7778
4.3	1387	1799	2205	2515	3028	3909	4831	6719	7963
4.4	1419	1841	2256	2573	3099	4000	4944	6875	8148
4.5	1452	1883	2308	2632	3169	4091	5056	7031	8333
4.6	1484	1925	2359	2690	3239	4182	5169	7188	8519
4.7	1516	1967	2410	2749	3310	4273	5281	7344	8704
4.8	1548	2008	2462	2807	3380	4364	5393	7500	8889
4.9	1581	2050	2513	2865	3451	4455	5506	7656	9074
5	1613	2092	2564	2924	3521	4545	5618	7813	9259
5.1	1645	2134	2615	2982	3592	4636	5730	7969	9444

TABLE 11 Fuse Voltage Drop Chart—Maxi Fuse *(continued)*

Fuse Voltage Drop Chart - Maxi Fuse
Circuit Current Across Fuse (milliAmps)

Fuse Color	Yellow	Grey	Green	Blu-Green	Orange	Red	Blue	Tan	Clear
Measurement mV	Maxi 20 Amp	Maxi 25 Amp	Maxi 30 Amp	Maxi 35 Amp	Maxi 40 Amp	Maxi 50 Amp	Maxi 60 Amp	Maxi 70 Amp	Maxi 80 Amp
5.2	1677	2176	2667	3041	3662	4727	5843	8125	9630
5.3	1710	2218	2718	3099	3732	4818	5955	8281	9815
5.4	1742	2259	2769	3158	3803	4909	6067	8438	10000
5.5	1774	2301	2821	3216	3873	5000	6180	8594	10185
5.6	1806	2343	2872	3275	3944	5091	6292	8750	10370
5.7	1839	2385	2923	3333	4014	5182	6404	8906	10556
5.8	1871	2427	2974	3392	4085	5273	6517	9063	10741
5.9	1903	2469	3026	3450	4155	5364	6629	9219	10926
6	1935	2510	3077	3509	4225	5455	6742	9375	11111
6.1	1968	2552	3128	3567	4296	5545	6854	9531	11296
6.2	2000	2594	3179	3626	4366	5636	6966	9688	11481
6.3	2032	2636	3231	3684	4437	5727	7079	9844	11667
6.4	2065	2678	3282	3743	4507	5818	7191	10000	11852
6.5	2097	2720	3333	3801	4577	5909	7303	10156	12037
6.6	2129	2762	3385	3860	4648	6000	7416	10313	12222
6.7	2161	2803	3436	3918	4718	6091	7528	10469	12407
6.8	2194	2845	3487	3977	4789	6182	7640	10625	12593
6.9	2226	2887	3538	4035	4859	6273	7753	10781	12778
7	2258	2929	3590	4094	4930	6364	7865	10938	12963
7.1	2290	2971	3641	4152	5000	6455	7978	11094	13148
7.2	2323	3013	3692	4211	5070	6545	8090	11250	13333
7.3	2355	3054	3744	4269	5141	6636	8202	11406	13519
7.4	2387	3096	3795	4327	5211	6727	8315	11563	13704
7.5	2419	3138	3846	4386	5282	6818	8427	11719	13889
7.6	2452	3180	3897	4444	5352	6909	8539	11875	14074
7.7	2484	3222	3949	4503	5423	7000	8652	12031	14259
7.8	2516	3264	4000	4561	5493	7091	8764	12188	14444
7.9	2548	3305	4051	4620	5563	7182	8876	12344	14630
8	2581	3347	4103	4678	5634	7273	8989	12500	14815
8.1	2613	3389	4154	4737	5704	7364	9101	12656	15000
8.2	2645	3431	4205	4795	5775	7455	9213	12813	15185
8.3	2677	3473	4256	4854	5845	7545	9326	12969	15370
8.4	2710	3515	4308	4912	5915	7636	9438	13125	15556
8.5	2742	3556	4359	4971	5986	7727	9551	13281	15741
8.6	2774	3598	4410	5029	6056	7818	9663	13438	15926
8.7	2806	3640	4462	5088	6127	7909	9775	13594	16111
8.8	2839	3682	4513	5146	6197	8000	9888	13750	16296
8.9	2871	3724	4564	5205	6268	8091	10000	13906	16481
9	2903	3766	4615	5263	6338	8182	10112	14063	16667
9.1	2935	3808	4667	5322	6408	8273	10225	14219	16852
9.2	2968	3849	4718	5380	6479	8364	10337	14375	17037
9.3	3000	3891	4769	5439	6549	8455	10449	14531	17222
9.4	3032	3933	4821	5497	6620	8545	10562	14688	17407
9.5	3065	3975	4872	5556	6690	8636	10674	14844	17593
9.6	3097	4017	4923	5614	6761	8727	10787	15000	17778
9.7	3129	4059	4974	5673	6831	8818	10899	15156	17963
9.8	3161	4100	5026	5731	6901	8909	11011	15313	18148
9.9	3194	4142	5077	5789	6972	9000	11124	15469	18333
10	3226	4184	5128	5848	7042	9091	11236	15625	18519

Voltage Drop Tests

Procedure—Positive Side

The procedure for a positive side voltage drop test is shown in **FIGURE 88**:

1. Run the engine at 2000 RPM.
2. Turn all electrical loads on except for the rear window defogger.
3. Set the meter to the DC volts scale.
4. Place the positive meter lead on the alternator B+ stud and the negative meter lead on the positive battery post.
5. The reading should not exceed 0.5 V DC.

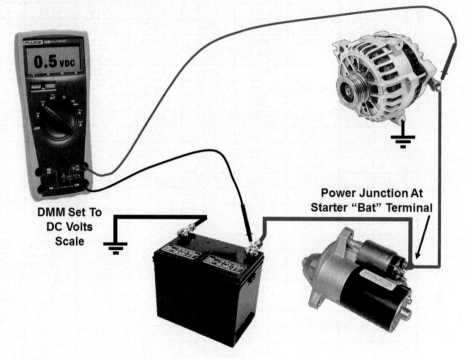

FIGURE 88 Positive side voltage drop test.

Procedure—Negative Side

The procedure for a negative side voltage drop test is shown in **FIGURE 89**:

1. Run the engine at 2000 RPM.
2. Turn all electrical loads on except for the rear window defogger.
3. Set the meter to the DC volts scale.
4. Place the positive meter lead on the negative battery post and the negative meter lead on the alternator case.
5. The reading should not exceed 0.3 V DC.

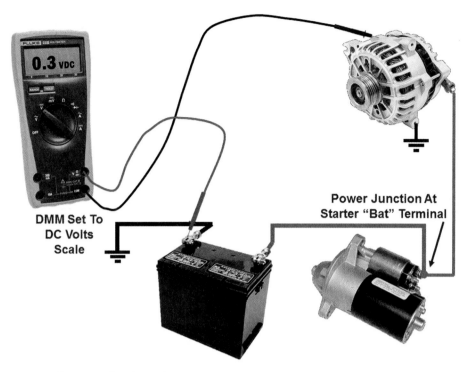

FIGURE 89 Negative side voltage drop test.

Results

If the voltage drop readings are within normal ranges, then excessive resistance is not the cause of the low alternator output. If voltage drop readings are too high, the cause must be corrected or the alternator output will continue to be low. See the pinpoint testing procedures.

Procedure—Pinpoint Testing

Current must be flowing for pinpoint voltage drop tests to work. This is accomplished by running the engine with the loads turned on or with a carbon pile connected across the alternator to produce the amp load (**FIGURE 90**).

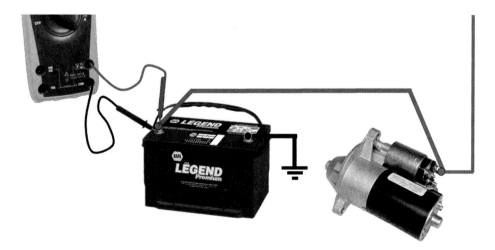

FIGURE 90 Pinpoint voltage drop testing.

Voltage drop between a battery post and cable end should be near zero.

Voltage drop across a battery cable should not exceed 0.2 V.

Voltage drop across a B+ harness should not exceed 0.2 V (**FIGURE 91**).

Voltage drop between the alternator case and the engine block should not exceed 0.1 V (**FIGURE 92**).

Voltage drop across a connection should not exceed 0.1 V (**FIGURE 93**).

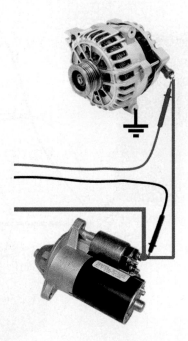

FIGURE 91 Voltage drop across a B+ harness.

Power Junction At Starter "Bat" Terminal

FIGURE 92 Voltage drop between the alternator case and engine block.

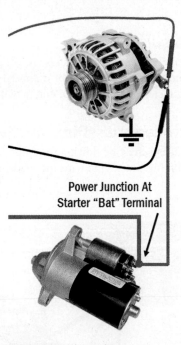

Power Junction At Starter "Bat" Terminal

FIGURE 93 Voltage drop across a connection.

Result

If voltage drop readings are too high, the excessive resistance must be removed or the alternator output will continue to be reduced.

Excessive AC Ripple Voltage Test

In addition to poor charging system performance, excessive AC ripple voltage can cause false trouble codes to be displayed and computer network communication errors (U codes).

Excessive AC ripple voltage is caused by faulty alternator diodes or output circuit issues. The 3-minute testing procedure will scan for and find excessive AC ripple voltage. The following is an additional check for finding excessive AC ripple voltage (**FIGURE 94**).

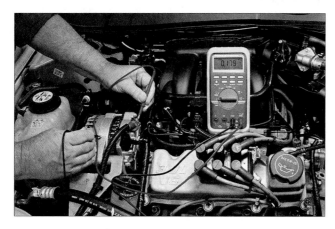

FIGURE 94 Testing for excessive AC ripple voltage.

Procedure

1. Set the meter to the AC volts scale.
2. Run the engine at idle RPM.
3. Apply 25 A load by only turning on the headlights.
4. Place the positive meter lead on the alternator B+ terminal and the negative meter lead on the alternator housing.

Results

The reading should not exceed 0.5 V AC. Some applications should not exceed 0.3 V AC. If it does exceed 0.5 V AC, the alternator needs to be replaced.

Alternator AC Ripple without ECM Control Test

The purpose of this test is to check the rectification of the alternator output voltage where the alternator output is not regulated by the ECM.

Procedure

1. Connect PicoScope Channel A to the alternator B+ terminal (**FIGURE 95**).
2. Minimize the Help page. You will see that PicoScope has displayed an example waveform and is preset to capture your waveform.
3. Start the engine and allow it to idle.
4. Start the scope to see live data.
5. Switch on electrical consumers and increase engine RPM while observing your waveform.
6. With your waveform on screen, stop the scope.
7. Turn off the engine.
8. Use the Waveform Buffer, Zoom, and Measurements tools to examine your waveform.

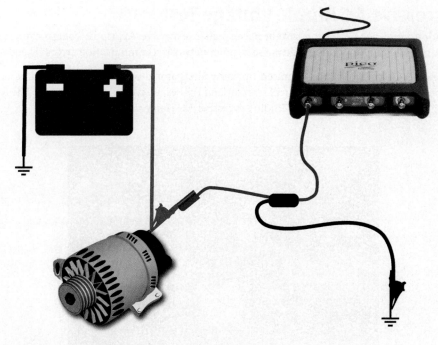

FIGURE 95 Testing connections.

Understanding the Waveform

The waveform in **FIGURE 96** has the following characteristics:

- An average voltage centered around 0 V (due to the AC coupling of the scope)
- A continuous series of ripples having a consistent amplitude
- No excessive or uneven downward spikes between ripple pulses
- No repetitively missing ripples or anomalies, where there are the same number of good ripples between each occurrence
- Potentially some noise spikes or voltage jumps, but their appearance should be random, not regular, after a fixed number of pulses

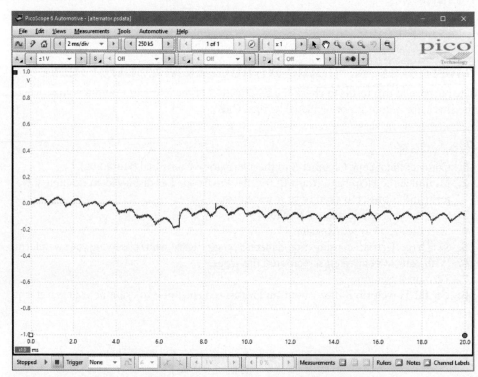

FIGURE 96 Sample of a good waveform.

To access the waveform library, go to the drop-down menu bar at the lower left corner of the **Waveform Library** window and select *Alternator ripple/diode test*.

Further Guidance

Consider the following points when testing the rectification of the alternator output voltage where the alternator output is not regulated by the ECM:

- When the engine is running, an alternator generates electrical energy to supply the vehicle's on-board electrical systems and replace the battery charge consumed during cranking.
- The alternator converts mechanical rotation to electrical energy by causing a magnetic field to rotate within a fixed set of windings. The changing magnetic field induces AC voltages within the windings, which are rectified by an arrangement of diodes to give a DC output.
- The maximum output is limited by a voltage regulator, which varies the alternator output relative to the system voltage. When the system voltage is low, the regulator increases the alternator output, and vice versa.
- The rectification of the generated AC creates a continuous series of voltage pulses (a ripple) within the alternator's output. Periodically missing pulses or disruptions within the ripple indicate a problem with either the windings or the rectification diodes. Sharp spikes, usually downward, between the pulses indicate diode failure and the presence of unrectified AC voltage in the circuitry.
- The alternator output will vary with engine speed and electrical load. However, a consistent ripple must be maintained throughout these variations.
- Turning on electrical consumers and increasing the engine speed increase the alternator load, which can provoke faults that are not evident at low loads. If the peak-to-peak output voltages are above 500 mV, the offending voltage spikes may disrupt other electrical systems, in particular those systems dependent on an AC signal.
- For an accurate and reliable signal, always connect at the alternator B+ terminal. It is convenient to measure the ripple directly at the battery positive terminal; however, the battery can dampen the waveform to the point where problems can be missed.
- Typical symptoms of a faulty alternator would be:
  - Battery warning light illumination
  - MIL illumination
  - DTCs
  - Rough idle
  - Possible engine misfire
  - Loss of battery state of charge or state of health
  - Erratic or malfunctioning dashboard instrumentation
- Alternator or related faults that can cause these symptoms include the following:
  - Diode faults caused by heat and vibration or the inclusion of moisture into the circuitry
  - Short or open circuits, or high resistances, in the stator windings
  - Poor battery states of health or charge
  - Short or open circuits, or high resistances, in battery or earth cables and/or connections
  - Alternator drive mechanism faults, including pulley, belt condition and tension, or freewheel issues

Relevant DTCs are listed in **TABLE 12**.

TABLE 12 Selection of Component-Related DTCs (Alternator AC Ripple)

P0620
P0621
P0622
P0623
P0624
P0625
P0626

NOTES

NOTES

Voltage "Sense" and Overcharging in the Computer

Procedure

1. Connect a scan tool to the vehicle (**FIGURE 97**).
2. Access the battery voltage PID (**FIGURE 98**).
3. Connect a voltmeter across the battery.
4. Compare the voltmeter and scan tool readings.

FIGURE 97 Scanner.   **FIGURE 98** DVOM.

Results

If the readings vary more than 0.2 V, an overcharge condition will result. The farther apart the readings are, the greater the overcharge will be. To correct the problem, use a wiring diagram and locate where the sense or voltage input circuit is picking up the battery voltage reading. Look for damage or corrosion in the sense or voltage input circuit. Also make sure that the computer module is properly grounded.

Ford PCM Communication Check

Procedure

1. Set a scope or properly equipped DVOM to the duty cycle function.
2. Using a backprobe, connect the positive scope or DVOM lead to the I or RC connector (yellow wire in **FIGURE 99**) at the voltage regulator harness plug on the alternator. Connect the negative scope or DVOM lead to the battery negative.
3. Start and run the engine at cruising RPM.
4. With the engine running, turn on heavy electrical loads, such as headlights, blowers, and rear window defoggers.
5. Monitor the scope or DVOM readings to see whether the duty cycle reading varies with the load changes.

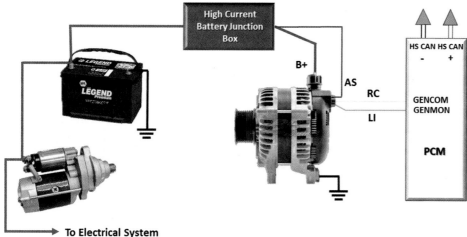

FIGURE 99 Ford PCM communication check.

If the duty cycle commands are varying with the load changes but the alternator output does not change, the voltage regulator is bad and the alternator needs to be replaced.

If there is no change in the duty cycle commands as the loads are varied, there may be a problem with the harness between the voltage regulator plug and the PCM or a problem may exist with the PCM itself. Verify the harness and/or PCM as follows:

1. Move the positive scope or meter lead from the I or RC connection at the voltage regulator plug to the I or RC harness connection at the PCM.
2. With the engine running at cruising RPM, vary the electrical loads while monitoring the duty cycle commands on the scope or DVOM.

If the duty cycle commands vary with load changes at the PCM connection, but not at the voltage regulator connection, there is a fault in the harness. If the duty cycle does not change at the PCM connection, there is a problem with the PCM operation.

Ford Alternator Smart Charge Test

The purpose of this test is to check the command, feedback, and output voltage signals from a Ford-type smart charging alternator.

Procedure

1. Use the manufacturer's data to identify the alternator command, feedback, and output circuits.
2. Connect the high amp clamp into PicoScope Channel A, select the 200 A range, and zero the clamp (**FIGURE 100**).
3. Connect the high amp clamp around the alternator B+ cable.
4. Connect PicoScope Channel B to the alternator feedback circuit.
5. Connect PicoScope Channel C to the alternator command circuit.
6. Start the engine and allow it to idle.
7. Minimize the Help page. You will see that PicoScope has displayed an example waveform and is preset to capture your waveform.
8. Start the scope to see live data.
9. Switch on electrical consumers and vary engine RPM while observing your waveforms.
10. With your waveforms on screen, stop the scope.
11. Stop the engine.
12. Use the Waveform Buffer, Zoom, and Measurements tools to examine your waveform.

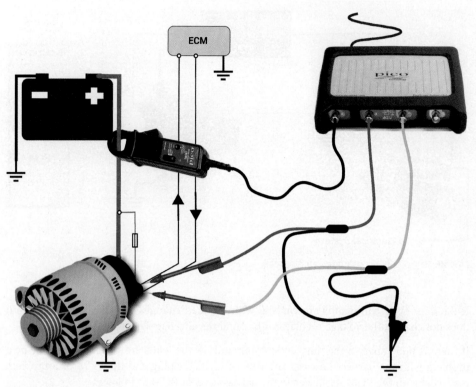

FIGURE 100 Test connections.

Understanding the Waveform

The known good waveforms in **FIGURES 101** and **102** have the following characteristics:

- At low loads, the alternator output current Channel A is approximately 14 A. With additional electrical loads, such as those from the heated seats, main beam headlights, and heater blower, the output current increases to 70 A.
- The alternator feedback signal Channel B is a PWM voltage waveform dependent on the alternator current output: with a low load, the waveform is around 0 V for approximately 60% of its cycle duration; at high loads, it is around 12 V for approximately 100% of its cycle duration.
- The alternator command signal from the ECM Channel C is a positive-switched PWM voltage waveform. With no load, it remains off, at 0 V. With moderate electrical loads, it is around 13 V for approximately 63% of its cycle duration.

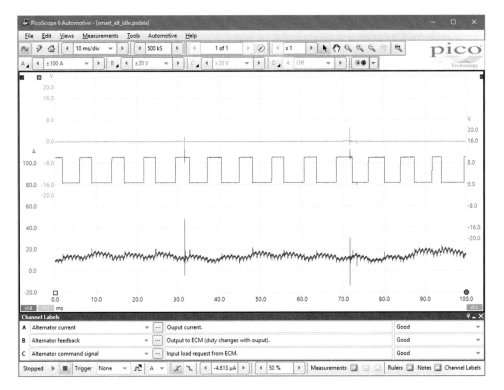

FIGURE 101 Engine at idle, alternator under light load.

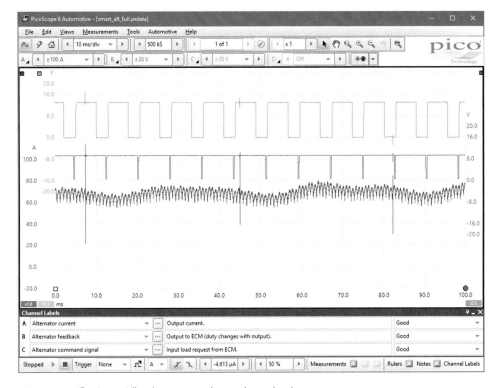

FIGURE 102 Engine at idle, alternator under moderate load.

To access the waveform library, go to the drop-down menu bar at the lower left corner of the **Waveform Library** window and select *Alternator command signal*, *Alternator feedback*, or *Alternator current*.

Further Guidance

Consider the following points when conducting a Ford alternator smart charge test:

- When the engine is running, an alternator generates electrical energy to supply the vehicle's on-board electrical systems and replace the battery charge consumed during cranking.
- Smart charge systems are able to balance these requirements against the needs of the driver, such as the requirement for maximum torque on hard acceleration and the need for less engine drag during normal operation, for better fuel efficiency. Furthermore, they can closely manage the battery's needs—for example, by providing a higher charging rate at cold ambient temperatures. This helps keep the battery in optimum states of charge and health.
- Typically, the ECM controls charging and can vary the charge rate dependent on several factors, such as ambient temperature (or battery ambient temperature), accelerator pedal position, electrical loading, and engine speed.
- The alternator works at maximum capacity only when absolutely necessary. However, in the right conditions, such as after cold cranking in low ambient temperatures, the ECM can increase alternator output to 18 V. Therefore, it is essential that correctly specified batteries are used in these applications. (Ford specified silver calcium batteries for their systems.)
- **Caution:** Conventional lead acid batteries, which cannot handle high charging rates, are not a suitable alternative in smart charging systems.
- Nowadays, smart charging systems are ubiquitous, but Ford was the first to add the feature to mass-market vehicles.
- Smart charge alternators have a similar fundamental design as conventional alternators, with an electromagnetic rotor within stator windings, but their output is regulated by smart control of the rotors' electromagnetic field: the ECM uses a PWM voltage signal to vary the rotor circuit current and, hence, its magnetic field strength. The higher its magnetic field, the higher the AC current induced in the stator windings and the higher the alternator's rectified DC output.
- A feedback signal is sent from the alternator to the ECM to provide a check that the system is operating within tolerance. For this reason, smart charge systems (notably, the Ford system) can be highly intolerant to any alternator that is not manufactured to the original specifications.
- If the smart alternator controller detects a system fault, the smart charging functionality is disabled, DTCs set, and the engine management and battery warning lights illuminated. Provided the fault is not within the alternator, it will still function conventionally with its output regulated to 14.75 V.
- Other possible symptoms of a faulty alternator or charging system might be:
  - Rough idle
  - Possible engine misfire
  - Loss of battery state of charge or state of health
  - Erratic or malfunctioning dashboard instrumentation
- Typical alternator or related faults are:
  - Diode faults, caused by heat and vibration or the inclusion of moisture into the circuitry
  - Short or open circuits, or high resistances, in the stator windings
  - Poor battery states of health or charge
  - Short or open circuits, or high resistances, in battery or earth cables and/or connections
  - Alternator drive mechanism faults, including pulley, belt condition and tension, or freewheel issues (**FIGURE 103**)

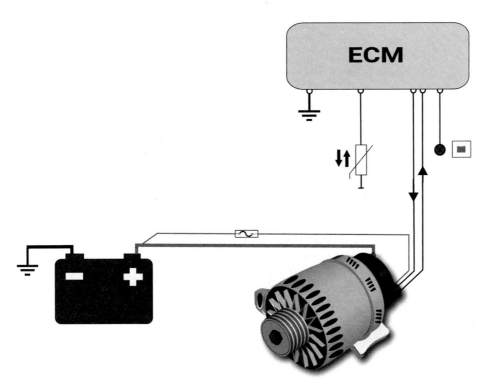

FIGURE 103 Pico test.

Chrysler No Charge Check

First, test the battery as described in this manual and detailed in the ESP Standard Manual. Check also for belt wear and slippage as described in this manual.

Procedure 1

1. With the engine off, check for battery voltage between the alternator B+ terminal and the alternator case.
2. If battery voltage is present, proceed to Procedure 2.
3. If there is no voltage present, check for an open in the B+ harness, fuse, or fusible link. Also verify that the alternator is properly grounded to the vehicle. This can be done by conducting a running voltage drop test between the alternator case and ground. Repair any problems that are found and retest.

Procedure 2

Using a wiring diagram and a voltmeter, perform a KOEO field circuit test:

1. Turn the key on but don't start the engine.
2. If necessary, use a scan tool to activate the computer field circuit.
3. Using a black probe, check for voltage at both field circuit connectors at the back of the alternator (**FIGURE 104**).

NOTES

FIGURE 104 Backprobe.

Results

If there is no voltage at either terminal, look for an opening or fault between terminal 1 and the field circuit power source. The problem could be faulty wiring. Depending on the vehicle, the problem could also be a bad power distribution module or a bad PCM.

If there is voltage at one terminal but not at the other, then there is an opening in the alternator field circuit and the alternator needs to be replaced.

If there is voltage at both terminals, check for a good terminal 2 connection to the PCM or to ground, depending on the wiring diagram information for the vehicle being checked. If the wiring connections are good, check for proper PCM operation. Remember that the PCM is the voltage regulator for all Chrysler applications built from the mid- to late 1990s to the present.

Verifying Computer Duty Cycle Response to Changing Electrical Loads

Procedure

Using an appropriate scanner, monitor duty cycle commands to the voltage regulator and voltage regulator feedback to the computer.

Perform this check by applying and removing heavy loads to the electrical system.

Monitor the Command (L for GM) and Feedback (F for GM) circuit responses while turning electrical loads on and off.

Result

If duty cycle commands are not varying with electrical load changes, then the computer is not responding to the changing electrical demands. Look for computer or software issues.

Duty Cycle Command Verification—Multimeter Method

Verify that the duty cycle commands are reaching the voltage regulator using a digital multimeter with a duty cycle function (**FIGURE 105**).

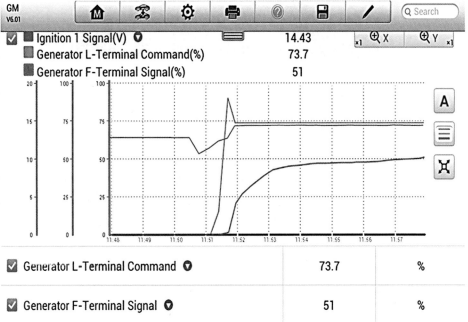

FIGURE 105 Graphing data.

Procedure

If the system is overcharging, verify voltage input information by comparing the battery voltage PID with an actual voltage reading at the battery. If there are no voltage input issues, proceed to the following steps:

If the charging system is not responding to load changes but the scanner command and feedback circuit readings are changing as electrical loads are varied, perform the following test to see whether duty cycle commands are reaching the voltage regulator:

1. Set the DVOM to the duty cycle function.
2. Using a backprobe, connect the positive meter lead to the command terminal connection on the voltage regulator harness (**FIGURE 106**).
3. Connect the negative meter lead to the negative battery (**FIGURE 107**).
4. Start and run the engine at 2000 RPM.
5. Observe the readings while applying and removing heavy vehicle electrical loads.

NOTES

FIGURE 106 Backprobe.

FIGURE 107 Negative post connection.

Results

If the duty cycle readings vary with the load changes but the alternator output is not changing, then the alternator is bad.

If the duty cycle readings are not changing with the load changes, look for a faulty command circuit or a computer issue (**FIGURES 108** and **109**).

FIGURE 108 Duty cycle at low electrical loading.

FIGURE 109 Duty cycle at high electrical loading.

Intermittent Command Circuit Failure Check

Procedure

1. Check for loose connections, particularly at the voltage regulator harness plug.
2. Connect a scanner and monitor command circuit operation.
3. While monitoring the command circuit operation, manually wiggle the harness connector and/or use a backprobe to wiggle the wire connection in the harness plug.

Results

If the command circuit data drop off while wiggling the harness plug or wires, there is a loose connection in the harness connector.

Repair or replace the harness connector to correct the problem.

Acronyms

AAT ambient air temperature

AC alternating current

AGM absorbable glass mat

APP accelerator pedal position

ASD automatic shutdown

BCM body control module

BTS battery temperature sensor

CAN controller area network

CCA cold cranking amps

CMP camshaft position

DC direct current

DLC data link connector

DTC diagnostic trouble code

DVOM digital volt ohm meter

ECM engine control module

ECT engine coolant temperature

EEC electronic engine control

FLA flooded lead acid

GBCM generator battery control module

GENCOM generator command

GENLI generator load input

GENMON generator monitor

GENRC generator regulator command

HS CAN high-speed controller area network

HSD high side driver

HVAC heating, ventilation, and air conditioning

IAT intake air temperature

IBS intelligent battery sensor

IOD ignition-off draw

IPC instrument panel cluster

JTEC jeep/truck engine controller

KOEO key on/engine off

LAN local area network

LED light-emitting diode

LIN local interconnect network

LSD low side driver

MAP manifold absolute pressure

MIL malfunction indicator lamp

MY model year

NGC next-generation controller

OBD on-board diagnostics

OBD-II on-board diagnostics second generation

OEM original equipment manufacturer

PCM powertrain control module

PDC power distribution center

PID parameter ID

PWM pulse width modulation

RPM revolutions per minute

RVC regulated voltage control

SARVC stand-alone RVC

SBEC single-board engine controller

SOC state of charge

TSB technical service bulletin

VPWR vehicle power

VSS vehicle speed sensor

NOTES

NOTES

Domestic Smart Charging Systems   91

NOTES

NOTES

NOTES

NOTES